EAT MORE VEG

EAT MORE VEG

ANNIE RIGG

National Trust

First published in the United Kingdom in 2020 by
National Trust Books
43 Great Ormond Street
London WC1N 3HZ

An imprint of Pavilion Books Company Ltd

ISBN: 9781911358879

A CIP catalogue record for this book is available from the British Library.

10 9 8 7 6 5 4 3 2 1

Reproduction by Rival Colour Ltd, UK
Printed by 1010 Printing International Ltd, China

Photographer: Nassima Rothacker
Home Economist: Annie Rigg
Prop Stylist: Alex Breeze
Creative Director: Helen Lewis
Senior Commissioning Editor: Peter Taylor
Senior Editor: Lucy Smith
Senior Designer: Gemma Doyle

With thanks to Maria Aversa, Lucinda Notley and Becks Wilkinson for their help on
the photoshoot.

This book is available at National Trust shops and online at www.nationaltrustbooks.
co.uk, or try the publisher (www.pavilionbooks.com) or your local bookshop.

CONTENTS

INTRODUCTION

This book is full of recipes in which vegetables are the shining stars, the heroes and the champions.

With recipes ranging from simple mid-week suppers, such as Indian-inspired Masala Omelette (page 29), to dishes for slower cooking, weekend entertaining and cooking for larger numbers, such as Golden Spiced Root Veg Tagine (page 83), these recipes cross continents and seasons. Simple side dishes, warming soups and colourful salads — all of these flavoursome recipes are vegetarian or vegan, with no meat substitutes, and are suited to those following a diet rich in vegetables or those who simply want to eat meat-free on certain days of the week and are in need of inspiration.

The chapters are divided into meal type, from starters and soups through to main courses, as well as recipes for when you want to pull out all the stops and those for when you want a simple snack. Within each chapter you'll find recipes using vegetables for all seasons. And that's one of the joys of cooking with fresh produce and vegetables — it's an ever-turning circle with each season bringing new flavours, textures and colours to your cooking. To get the best flavour (and value for money) you need to cook with what's best in any given season. And consider those food miles for environmental, financial and flavour reasons — those tomatoes flown halfway around the world in December are going to be twice the price and have half as much flavour as those grown locally in July.

Almost all of the ingredients in this book, whether fresh or store-cupboard items, can be found in most decent-sized supermarkets or online. Look out for the best seasonal produce at your local farmers' market and support your local greengrocer. If you're lucky enough to have your own allotment or veg garden, then you might be faced with a glut of tomatoes, potatoes or beans and be looking for ideas to use them up.

Whether you are following a plant-based, vegetarian or vegan diet for health or environmental reasons, you will need to be aware of the importance of incorporating enough protein into your diet. This is normally found in meat, dairy, fish and eggs, but can easily and deliciously be found in pulses, grains, nuts and seeds. Bags of freekeh, spelt, bulgur wheat, chickpeas, lentils and beans — both tinned and dried — are store-cupboard essentials. They are also fabulous partners to vegetables, both nutritionally and as a means of adding flavour and texture.

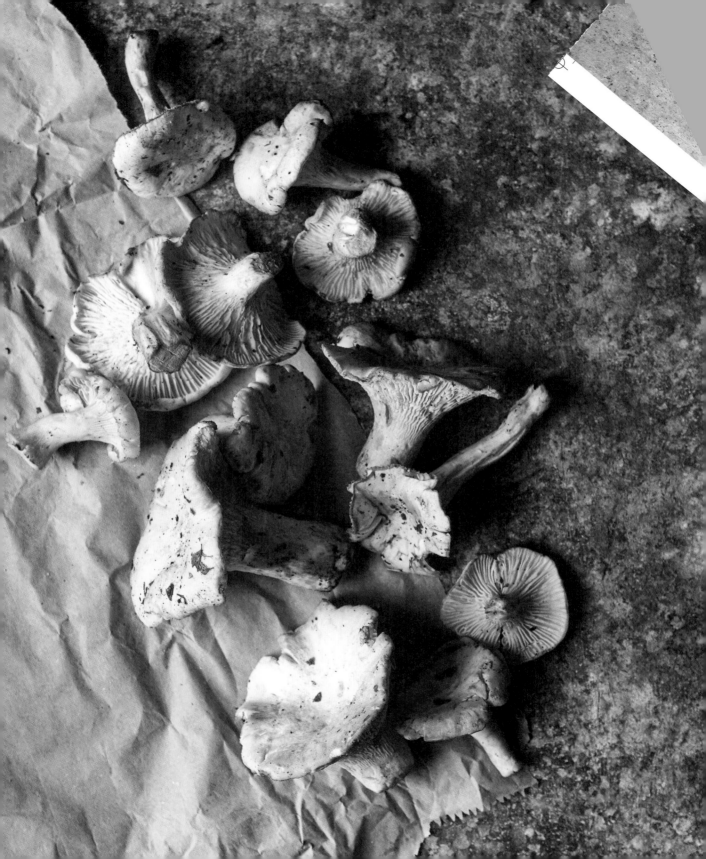

Vegetables love a bit of spice and a good handful of fresh herbs. Both are used liberally throughout this book. Spices enhance and enrich your cooking, providing warmth, depth, aroma and sweetness. Soft herbs, such as parsley, mint and coriander, add lightness and are often added at the end of cooking, while bay, rosemary, thyme and sage provide an extra depth of flavour and are mostly used during cooking. You don't need to have jars of every spice under the sun but a relatively small selection. Those used most regularly in my kitchen (and in this book) include aromatic spices such as coriander seeds, cumin seeds, ground turmeric, hot and spicy cayenne, paprika and crushed dried chillies as well as warming fennel and mustard seeds. I also prefer to buy bags of black peppercorns and grind them myself and use sea-salt flakes rather than table salt. Many of the recipes in this book take influences from Indian, South East Asian and North African cooking, where spices and herbs play an important role in the cuisines, and vegetables and vegetarian cooking are celebrated.

Vegetarian cooking has come of age. We are light years away from nut roasts and risotto — although you will find a risotto, as well as a delicious twist using pearled spelt and beetroot, within these pages. You'll also find sumptuous braises using a rainbow of tomatoes, fennel and chickpeas, punchy salads of raw carrots enlivened with herbs, spices and preserved lemons, and a comforting onion soup with indulgent and moreish cheese croutons.

If you are following a vegetarian diet you will need to be aware that some cheeses (such as Parmesan or Parmigiano-Reggiano, Pecorino, Grana Padano, Taleggio, Comté, Roquefort and Gorgonzola) are never vegetarian as they contain animal rennet as a processing ingredient. However, most supermarkets sell Italian-style hard cheese as a good vegetarian alternative to Parmesan and other blue cheeses to those listed above — but do check the labels to be sure. If you're simply trying to incorporate more veg into your diet rather than following a vegetarian diet, you can use either.

Always use unwaxed citrus fruit in vegan cooking — the coating on waxed fruit can be derived from beeswax or shellac, so it's best to err on the side of caution. If waxed fruits are your only option, be sure to scrub them well in hot water before grating any zest. Please also check whether cooking wine is vegan before using it. Eggs should always be free-range and preferably organic.

There are recipes here to suit all levels of cook. Whether you are switching to a plant-based diet or have been veggie for years, hopefully these recipes will encourage and inspire you to eat more veg!

QUICK SUPPERS

Delicious and easy supper dishes — packed with veggies and full of flavour, from veg fried rice, and loaded open sandwiches to fritters and quick braises.

ROOT VEGETABLE ROSTI

You can try swapping the celeriac or parsnips for beetroot, if you like, but keep the potato ratio as the potatoes provide much needed starch that helps the mixture hold together. This rosti is delicious topped with a fried egg (if not cooking a vegan version) and some sautéed garlicky rainbow chard.

MAKES 12 SMALL ROSTI

**150g red-skinned potatoes,
    such as Désirée**
**100g parsnip (roughly
    1 parsnip)**
**100g celeriac (roughly
    ¼ celeriac)**
**100g carrot (roughly
    1 medium carrot)**
1 small onion
1 clove garlic, crushed
2 tbsp chopped parsley
1 tbsp plain flour
2 tbsp sunflower oil
**salt and freshly ground
    black pepper**

Coarsely grate the potatoes, parsnip, celeriac and carrot onto a clean tea towel. Finely slice the onion, add to the veg and gather the tea towel into a pouch encasing the vegetables. Squeeze the tea towel around the veg and over the sink to squeeze out any excess moisture.

Tip the vegetables into a mixing bowl and add the crushed garlic, parsley and plain flour. Season well and, using clean hands, mix well to combine thoroughly. Heat half of the oil in a non-stick frying pan over a low-medium heat. Using your hands, shape half of the rosti mixture into 6 patties. Cook in the pan for about 5 minutes until golden on the underside. Carefully turn the rosti over and cook until golden on the other side. Remove from the pan and keep warm while you cook the remaining mixture in the remaining oil.

TIP Small rosti are great for children and small plates but if you prefer you can make 6 larger rosti, just remember you may need to increase the cooking time slightly. You could also make one large rosti if you are feeling brave and have a suitably sized non-stick pan. Once you've browned the rosti on both sides slide the (oven-proof) pan into a moderate oven for 10–15 minutes to ensure that the veggies are cooked through. If your pan isn't ovenproof, carefully turn the rosti out onto a baking tray first.

COURGETTE AND PEA FRITTERS
WITH FETA AND DILL

Serve these fritters with some garlicky greens, a spoonful of chunky houmous and lemon wedges for squeezing over. Any leftovers would be delicious in a lunch box with some pitta bread and sliced tomatoes.

SERVES 4

1 large courgette

100g peas (fresh or frozen and defrosted)

2 spring onions, finely sliced

2 tbsp chopped flat-leaf parsley, plus extra to serve

1 tbsp chopped dill, plus extra to serve

1 clove garlic, crushed

100g feta, crumbled

¼ tsp cayenne pepper

75g plain flour

½ tsp baking powder

1 medium egg, lightly beaten

50ml milk

2–3 tbsp olive oil

salt and freshly ground black pepper

lemon wedges, to serve

Coarsely grate the courgette, squeeze dry in kitchen paper to remove any excess water and tip into a large bowl. You will need roughly 150g after squeezing dry. Add the peas, sliced spring onions, chopped herbs and crushed garlic.

Crumble the feta into the bowl, add the cayenne and season well with salt and freshly ground black pepper. Add the flour, baking powder, beaten egg and milk, and mix well to combine.

You will need to cook the fritters in batches. Heat half of the olive oil in a large frying pan over a low-medium heat and add the fritter mixture, one rounded tablespoonful at a time. Cook for about 2 minutes until golden brown and then turn over and cook the fritters on the other side until puffed, crisp and golden. Remove from the pan and keep warm while you add the remaining oil to the pan and cook the remaining mixture.

Serve with a tahini yoghurt dip (see tip), lemon wedges and a sprinkling of roughly chopped herbs.

TIP *Make a quick tahini yoghurt dip by stirring 3 tbsp tahini into 4 tbsp natural yoghurt, add a squeeze of lemon juice and season with salt and pepper. Loosen with a splash of water, if needed.*

BAKED EGGS
WITH TOMATOES AND SMOKY AUBERGINES

This flavoursome dish is a hybrid of shakshuka, a popular Middle Eastern dish of spiced stewed tomatoes (and sometimes red peppers) and egg, and zaalouk, a Moroccan smoky aubergine and cooked tomato salad. Together they make a winning combination for a midweek supper or weekend brunch.

SERVES 4

2 aubergines
3 tbsp fruity olive oil, plus
   extra to serve
1 large onion, sliced
1 red pepper, diced
2 fat cloves garlic, crushed
1 tbsp tomato purée
1 tsp harissa paste
1 rounded tsp ground
   cumin
1 tsp paprika
½ tsp Aleppo chilli flakes
½ tsp caster sugar, or to
   taste
8 ripe tomatoes, chopped
200g cooked chickpeas
4 eggs
100g crumbled feta
   (optional)
small handful roughly
   chopped coriander leaves
1 tbsp roughly chopped dill
salt and freshly ground
   black pepper
toasted pitta or warmed flat
   breads, to serve

Prick the aubergines with a skewer and place directly over a gas flame or barbecue and cook for about 12 minutes, turning often, until the skin is charred and the aubergine flesh is very soft inside (see tip). Leave the aubergines on a plate to cool while you prepare the remaining ingredients.

Heat the olive oil in a large sauté pan, add the sliced onion, diced pepper and crushed garlic, and cook over a low-medium heat for about 7 minutes until softened. Add the tomato purée, harissa, spices and sugar, and season with salt and freshly ground black pepper. Mix well and continue to cook for a further 2 minutes.

Add the chopped tomatoes and 250ml water, mix well to combine and continue to cook until the tomatoes have broken down and softened into a thick sauce. While the sauce is cooking, cut off the stalks, scrape the charred skin from the aubergines and roughly chop the soft flesh.

Add the aubergine and cooked chickpeas to the tomato pan and cook for another 5 minutes, adding a little more water if the sauce appears too dry. Taste the sauce and add more seasoning or sugar to taste.

Make 4 wells in the sauce using the back of the wooden spoon. Break one egg into each hole, scatter over the crumbled feta (if using) and season the eggs with salt and freshly ground black pepper. Continue to cook over a medium heat for about 5 minutes until the eggs are just cooked.

Remove from the heat, drizzle with a little olive oil, scatter with the chopped coriander and dill, and serve with toasted pitta or warmed flat breads.

TIP *The aubergines are best cooked directly over a gas flame or BBQ but if you have neither, simply dice them and sauté in olive oil until golden brown and tender before adding to the tomatoes.*

GREEN HOUMOUS
WITH MINTED LEMONY PEAS AND HALLOUMI

You can use either edamame or broad beans in this vibrant green houmous, but if using broad beans, do double-pod them after cooking. This is a light supper or lunch dish that can be made more substantial by serving some dolmades or falafel alongside.

SERVES 4

175g peas (frozen is fine)
75g podded edamame or
  broad beans
400g can chickpeas,
  drained and rinsed
1 large clove garlic, roughly
  chopped
1 rounded tbsp tahini
grated zest and juice of
  1 lemon
5 tbsp extra-virgin olive oil,
  plus extra to drizzle
2 tbsp chopped flat-leaf
  parsley
2 tbsp chopped mint, plus
  1–2 tbsp shredded mint
  leaves
40g pistachios, roughly
  chopped
2 tsp za'atar
2 handfuls baby spinach
  leaves or pea shoots
4 baby cucumbers,
  quartered
250g block halloumi cheese
1 tbsp olive oil
salt and freshly ground
  black pepper
toasted flat breads and
  pickled chillies, to serve

Start by making the houmous. It can be prepared ahead and chilled until needed. Cook the peas in boiling salted water for 1–2 minutes; remove from the pan with a slotted spoon and cool quickly under cold running water. Cook the edamame (or podded broad beans) in the same pan for 1 minute, drain and cool in the same way. Tip 75g peas and all of the beans into a food processor, add the drained chickpeas, chopped garlic, tahini and juice of ½ lemon. Add 3 tbsp extra-virgin olive oil, season well with salt and freshly ground black pepper, and blend until almost smooth. Add the chopped herbs and blend again. Taste and add more lemon juice and seasoning if needed. Spoon onto a serving platter, cover and chill until ready to serve.

Tip the remaining peas into a bowl, add the zest and juice of ½ lemon, the remaining 2 tbsp extra-virgin olive oil and the shredded mint. Season and mix to combine.

Drizzle the houmous with a little more extra-virgin olive oil, sprinkle with the chopped pistachios and za'atar, and spoon the minted peas alongside. Arrange the leaves and quartered cucumbers on the platter.

Remove the halloumi from its packaging, pat dry on kitchen paper and cut into 12 slices. Heat the olive oil in a non-stick frying pan over a medium-high heat, add the halloumi and fry quickly until golden brown on one side, then turn and cook the other side. You may need to cook the halloumi in batches depending on the size of your pan. Place the hot halloumi on the platter and serve with toasted flat breads and pickled green chillies.

BRAISED CANNELLINI BEANS
WITH ROASTED CHERRY TOMATOES AND GREENS

VEGAN

Serve this simply with some grilled sourdough bread for mopping up any juices. If you are not following a vegan diet you could grate some halloumi or crumble some feta over the top of each portion.

SERVES 4

1 onion
1 carrot
1 stick celery
1 small leek
4 tbsp fruity olive oil
1 fat clove garlic, crushed
1 tablespoon tomato purée
4 sun-dried tomatoes in oil, drained and finely chopped
400g can cannellini or flageolet beans, drained and rinsed
1 bay leaf
1 sprig rosemary
300ml vegetable stock
200g cherry tomatoes on the vine
100g kale or cavolo nero, trimmed and shredded
salt and freshly ground black pepper

Dice the onion, carrot, celery and leek, and tip into a medium-sized saucepan. Add 2 tbsp olive oil and cook over a low-medium heat for about 10 minutes, stirring often, until tender but not coloured. Add the crushed garlic, tomato purée and chopped sun-dried tomatoes, and continue to cook for a further minute.

Preheat the oven to 190°C/375°F/gas mark 5.

Add the drained beans, bay leaf, rosemary sprig and vegetable stock, season well with salt and freshly ground black pepper and bring to a gentle simmer. Cover with a lid and cook for 20 minutes until the beans are tender.

Meanwhile, place the tomatoes in a small roasting tin, drizzle over the remaining olive oil and season well with salt and freshly ground black pepper. Roast on the middle shelf of the hot oven for about 20 minutes until the tomatoes are softened and starting to burst their skins.

Stir the shredded kale or cavolo nero into the beans and cook for another minute or so until wilted.

Spoon the beans into bowls or on to plates, top with roasted cherry tomatoes and drizzle over any juices from the roasting tin.

SPICED VEG FRIED RICE

This is a super veg-laden version of a staple takeaway treat, which makes a filling and nutritious supper dish. The brown rice is cooked in advance and left to cool in the fridge — this stops the rice grains breaking up during stir-frying. A little bowl of vegan kimchi on the side wouldn't go amiss. This is available in good health-food stores.

SERVES 4

200g brown basmati rice
4 spring onions
2 medium carrots
200g tatsoi (see tip)
100g peas (fresh or frozen
  and defrosted)
2 large eggs
4 tsp soy sauce
2 tbsp sunflower oil
1 fat clove garlic, crushed
1 tsp grated ginger
½–1 red chilli, sliced
4 tsp sesame oil
2 tsp toasted or black
  sesame seeds

Cook the brown basmati rice in boiling water for about 25 minutes or until al dente. Drain the rice, refresh under cold running water and leave to dry on kitchen paper for about 5 minutes. Tip the rice into a bowl, cover and chill for at least 2 hours.

Prepare all of the remaining ingredients just before you are ready to cook and eat. Thinly slice the spring onions, cut the carrots into fine matchsticks, shred the tatsoi leaves and stems, and defrost the peas if frozen.

Beat the eggs with 1 tsp of the soy sauce. Heat half of the oil in a large non-stick frying pan or wok over a high heat, add the eggs, leave to set for 20 seconds and then scramble quickly using a fork to break up the egg. Remove from the pan and set aside. Heat the remaining oil in the pan, add the sliced spring onions, garlic, ginger and chilli, and stir-fry for 30 seconds. Tip the carrots and tatsoi into the pan and cook, stirring constantly, until the greens are just wilted. Add the rice, peas and remaining 3 tsp soy sauce to the pan and cook for a further 3 minutes until the rice is piping hot. Add the egg and stir to combine.

Spoon into bowls, drizzle with the sesame oil, scatter over the sesame seeds and serve immediately.

TIP *This recipe uses tatsoi, a leafy Asian green vegetable similar to pak choi. You could also use choy sum or Chinese leaf. A handful of shredded sugar snap peas, mangetout, red pepper, beansprouts or shitake mushrooms would also be great additions or substitutions.*

TOASTED OPEN SANDWICH
WITH CHARGRILLED VEG AND WHIPPED FETA

This is more than a sandwich — it's a meal in itself. Whipped feta cheese is a step up from more mild-mannered cream cheese which you could use at a pinch here. Try adding to or swapping the chargrilled veg for some roasted peppers or Puttanesca Cherry Tomatoes (see page 146) and switching the watercress to wild rocket or young leaf spinach.

SERVES 2

1 large aubergine
1 large courgette
3 tbsp fruity olive oil
1 large sprig thyme,
  leaves only
juice of ½ lemon
2 large, thick slices
  sourdough bread
1 clove garlic
200g feta
handful watercress sprigs
salt and freshly ground
  black pepper

GREEN OLIVE AND
PISTACHIO SALSA

2 tbsp pitted green olives
2 tbsp pistachios
2 tsp capers
1 tsp finely grated lemon
  zest
1 tbsp fruity olive oil
1 tbsp chopped parsley

Start by preparing the vegetables. Trim the aubergine and courgette and cut into 5mm–1cm thick slices. Preheat a ridged griddle pan over a medium-high heat.

Brush the courgette and aubergine slices with olive oil and cook on the ridged griddle pan until tender and nicely charred on both sides. Remove from the pan, season, scatter with the thyme leaves and drizzle with 1 tablespoon olive oil and the lemon juice. Set aside.

While the griddle pan is hot, toast the bread on both sides. Cut the garlic clove in half and rub over one side of the toast.

Crumble the feta into a mini food processor. Crush the remaining garlic clove half and add it to the food processor along with 1 tbsp olive oil. Season with pepper and whizz until smooth and creamy.

To make the salsa, finely chop the olives, pistachios and capers, and tip into a bowl. Add the finely grated lemon zest, olive oil and chopped parsley, season and mix to combine.

Spread the whipped feta onto the toast, top with a few watercress sprigs and top with the chargrilled vegetables. Spoon the olive and pistachio salsa over the top to serve.

SWEET POTATO CAKES
WITH AVOCADO

These lightly spiced sweet potato cakes can be prepared in advance, chilled and then fried when you are ready to serve. Try also serving them each with a poached egg and perhaps a drizzle of harissa or chermoula paste if you prefer things a little more spicy.

SERVES 4

550–600g sweet potatoes
  (about 3 medium
  potatoes)
1 onion
3 tbsp olive oil
1 large clove garlic, crushed
1 tsp grated ginger
1 green chilli, finely
  chopped
1 tsp cumin seeds
4 spring onions, sliced
2 tbsp chopped coriander
1 tbsp cornflour or potato
  flour
100g semolina, fine polenta
  or dried breadcrumbs
salt and freshly ground
  black pepper

TO SERVE

2 avocados, sliced
4 tbsp soured cream
2 tbsp sliced jalapenos or
  1 large red chilli, sliced
2 tbsp coriander leaves
1 lime, cut into wedges

Peel the sweet potatoes, chop into large chunks and cook in boiling salted water until just tender when tested with the point of a sharp knife. The potatoes should still have some give and texture.

While the potatoes are cooking, finely slice the onion and scoop it into a frying pan. Add 1 tbsp olive oil and cook over a low-medium heat for about 10 minutes until softened and just starting to caramelise at the edges. Add the crushed garlic, ginger, chopped chilli and cumin seeds, and cook for another minute before tipping into a large bowl.

Drain the potatoes thoroughly through a colander and then add to the bowl, mashing the potatoes with the back of a wooden spoon as you do so. Add the sliced spring onions, chopped coriander and cornflour, season well with salt and freshly ground black pepper, and mix to combine thoroughly – you may find it easier to use your hands if the mixture is cool enough.

Divide the mixture into 4 even portions and shape into balls. Flatten them into cakes about 2cm thick and leave on a baking sheet for 30 minutes to firm up. You can prepare the potato cakes up to this point, cover and chill until ready to coat and fry.

Coat the potato cakes in semolina, polenta or breadcrumbs and heat the remaining oil in a large frying pan over a medium heat. Add the potato cakes and cook on one side for 3 minutes until golden and then carefully flip the cakes over and cook the other side for a further 3 minutes until golden brown and heated through.

Serve each portion with sliced avocado, a spoonful of soured cream, some sliced chillies, coriander leaves and a lime wedge for squeezing over.

ASPARAGUS AND PSB LOADED SANDWICH
WITH OLIVES, RICOTTA AND ALMONDS

Sometimes all you want for lunch or supper is a sandwich. This open sandwich is up a notch up from the average cheese and tomato — and this one is with the unusual combination of asparagus and PSB (or purple sprouting broccoli). Look out for really good sourdough and ricotta. Sun-dried tomatoes are a wonderful standby ingredient to keep in your fridge, but if you happen to have some Puttanesca Cherry Tomatoes (see page 146), then so much the better.

SERVES 2

2 large slices sourdough
   bread
1 fat clove garlic
2 tbsp extra-virgin olive oil
150g purple sprouting
   broccoli, trimmed
8 spears asparagus,
   trimmed
150g ricotta
grated zest and juice of
   ½ lemon
2 tbsp mixed pitted olives,
   roughly chopped
2 tbsp sun-dried tomatoes,
   roughly chopped
25g salted and roasted
   almonds, roughly chopped
sea salt flakes and freshly
   ground black pepper

Preheat a grill or, better still, a ridged griddle pan. Toast the bread on both sides until nicely browned. Rub one side of each slice with the garlic, sprinkle with salt and drizzle with 1 tbsp extra-virgin olive oil then set aside.

Tip the broccoli and asparagus into a bowl and toss with the remaining oil. Season well and cook on the hot griddle pan or under the grill until the edges are nicely charred and the vegetables are tender.

Beat the ricotta until smooth, add the lemon zest and season with salt and freshly ground black pepper. Spread the ricotta on each slice of toast, top with the chargrilled vegetables and scatter over the olives, tomatoes and almonds. Serve with a squeeze of lemon juice.

ROASTED BUTTERNUT SQUASH 'CARBONARA'

Pangritata is often referred to as poor man's Parmesan — crisp seasoned breadcrumbs, they make a wonderful topping for pasta dishes, such as this vegan 'carbonara'. They can (and should) be made from day-old bread and ahead of time. Tahini is an unusual ingredient to use in pasta dishes but it does provide a creaminess, and the nutty flavour pairs well with roasted butternut squash.

SERVES 4

700g peeled and diced butternut squash
3 cloves garlic
2 sprigs fresh sage
3 tbsp fruity olive oil, plus extra to serve
½ tsp crushed dried chilli flakes
400g dried tagliatelle or fettuccine
3 tbsp tahini
2 tbsp chopped parsley

PANGRITATA

150g sourdough bread
2 tbsp olive oil
½ tsp crushed dried chilli flakes
½ tsp dried oregano
½ tsp garlic granules
salt and freshly ground black pepper

Preheat the oven to 190°C/375°F/gas mark 5.

Tip the diced squash, whole unpeeled garlic cloves and sage into a roasting tin, add the olive oil and chilli flakes, and season with plenty of salt and freshly ground black pepper. Mix to coat, cover with foil and then roast on the middle shelf of the preheated oven for about 30 minutes until the squash is tender. Remove the foil and cook for another 5–10 minutes until the squash is starting to turn golden brown at the edges.

While the squash is roasting, prepare the pangritata. Tear the bread into chunks and whizz in a food processor into crumbs — nothing too fine — the crumbs should still have some texture. Tip into a mixing bowl, add the remaining ingredients and mix well to combine. Scatter the crumbs onto a baking tray and cook on the shelf below the squash for about 20 minutes until crisp and golden, mixing halfway through baking so that they crisp evenly. Remove from the oven and leave to cool.

Bring a large pan of salted water to the boil and cook the pasta until al dente according to the pack instructions – usually 9–11 minutes. Use a ladle to remove and reserve 500ml of the cooking water, then drain the pasta and return it to the pan.

Tip half of the roasted butternut squash into a frying pan, add any residual olive oil from the roasting tin and squeeze in the flesh from the garlic. Cook over a medium heat, mashing the squash with the back of a wooden spoon. Add the tahini and 300ml of the pasta water and mix until smooth. Tip into the cooked pasta, add the remaining diced and roasted squash and mix well to coat, adding more pasta water to loosen the sauce if needed. Add the chopped parsley and season well with salt and freshly ground black pepper. Divide between bowls, drizzle with a little olive oil and top with the pangritata to serve.

MASALA OMELETTE

Potatoes and spinach are not normally added to this Indian staple breakfast dish, but they do add another portion of veggies to your daily quota and make it a more substantial supper dish. Serve it with warm roti, naan or paratha.

SERVES 2

6 small new potatoes

3 tbsp light olive or
   sunflower oil

½ tsp cumin seeds

4 eggs

3 spring onions, sliced

1 clove garlic, crushed

1 green chilli, finely
   chopped

2 tbsp chopped coriander

6 cherry tomatoes,
   quartered

½ tsp ground turmeric

½ tsp garam masala

good handful young leaf
   spinach

salt and freshly ground
   black pepper

Cook the potatoes in boiling salted water until tender when tested with the point of a knife. Drain and cut into quarters.

Heat half of the olive oil in a medium (20cm) frying pan over a medium heat, add the cooked potatoes and cook for 3–4 minutes until golden, turning often. Add the cumin seeds, season well with salt and freshly ground black pepper and, crushing the potatoes slightly with the back of the wooden spoon, cook for a further 2 minutes until crisp. Remove the potatoes from the pan.

Break the eggs into a bowl and mix to combine. Add the sliced spring onions, crushed garlic, chilli, coriander, cherry tomatoes, turmeric and garam masala, season and mix well to combine.

Heat the remaining oil in the pan over a medium heat and ladle in half of the egg mixture. Cook the omelette quickly, swirling the pan and dragging the edges of the omelette into the middle of the pan to allow the runny egg to fill the space. When the egg is almost set, add half of the potatoes and spinach to the pan and continue to cook for 1 minute. Slide the omelette onto a warm plate and cook the second omelette in the same way.

Serve immediately with warm roti, naan or paratha.

TIP *If you're planning on making this for Monday supper, cook a few extra spuds with your Sunday roast and use these instead of boiling new.*

MAINS

*Curries, stews, tarts, roasts and bakes
— delicious and nutritious vegetable dishes
more suited for when you've a little
time to linger, both in the kitchen
and at the dinner table.*

INDIAN-SPICED
ROASTED ROMANESCO
WITH CURRY LEAVES AND DAL

Dal is a delicious and hugely versatile lentil dish. It is easy to prepare and can be served as a side, on its own with some crispy fried onions and spices, or turned into a hearty meal with some roasted veggies as it has been here. Split red lentils are the easiest and quickest to use for dal as they require no pre-soaking or lengthy cooking. Serve with an assortment of Indian pickles and chutneys, and some minty yoghurt raita – use coconut yoghurt, if you prefer to keep this vegan.

SERVES 4

DAL

150g split red lentils
¼ tsp ground turmeric
1 small onion, sliced
1 clove garlic, sliced
1 slice fresh ginger
salt and freshly ground
 black pepper

ROMANESCO

1 romanesco cauliflower
1 tsp cumin seeds
1 tsp coriander seeds
1 tsp crushed dried chilli
 flakes
2 tbsp sunflower oil
2 tbsp flaked almonds
2 tbsp sultanas
2 tbsp pumpkin seeds
12 cherry tomatoes
salt and freshly ground
 black pepper

continues...

Start by making the dal, which can be prepared ahead of time and reheated when required. Tip the lentils into a sieve and rinse well under cold running water. Tip into a medium-large saucepan and add 1 litre cold water. Bring to the boil over a medium heat and use a slotted spoon to remove any scum that rises to the surface.

Add the turmeric, onion, garlic and ginger to the pan and reduce the heat to a very gentle simmer. Half-cover the pan with a lid and cook, stirring often, for about 40 minutes until the lentils have broken down, thickened and any remaining liquid has mostly been cooked off.

Remove the ginger slice, season well with salt and freshly ground black pepper and set aside until ready to reheat and serve.

Preheat the oven to 180°C/360°F/gas mark 4.

Cut the romanesco into florets and tip into a bowl. Lightly crush the cumin and coriander seeds using a pestle and mortar, then add to the cauliflower with the chilli flakes and sunflower oil. Season with salt and freshly ground black pepper, and mix well to combine. Tip onto a baking tray in a single layer and roast for about 20 minutes until starting to brown at the edges. Add the flaked almonds, sultanas, pumpkin seeds and cherry tomatoes and return to the oven for a further 5–10 minutes until the tomatoes are softened.

continues...

CURRY LEAVES

1 tbsp sunflower oil
1 tsp black mustard seeds
small handful curry leaves
2 cloves garlic, sliced
1 green chilli sliced

Meanwhile, start to gently reheat the dal and prepare the curry leaves. Heat 1 tbsp oil in a small frying pan, add the mustard seeds, curry leaves, sliced garlic and chilli, and cook over a medium-high heat until the mustard seeds pop, the curry leaves crisp and the garlic starts to turn golden.

Spoon the dal into bowls, add the roasted cauliflower, nuts, seeds and tomatoes, and top with the spiced curry leaves mixture to serve.

TIP *Romanesco is an old Italian cauliflower variety with bright green curds and a slightly sweet and nutty flavour. It is in season from late summer/early autumn to around December and is becoming more widely available with supermarkets catching on to its good looks and delicious flavour. If it is out of season or unavailable you could use a mixture of broccoli and regular cauliflower in this recipe.*

COURGETTE, PEA AND BASIL RISOTTO

This risotto has a high veg to rice ratio and should be more soupy than firm. Add some asparagus and young broad beans (outer skins removed). You could also swap young leaf spinach for wild garlic, if you're lucky enough to find some. For a special finish, you can garnish this dish with a handful of pea shoots dressed in a dash of lemon juice and extra-virgin olive oil.

SERVES 4

2 courgettes
2 tbsp olive oil
1 sprig thyme
1 onion, finely chopped
1 fat clove garlic, crushed
200g risotto rice
150ml dry white wine
1.2 litres hot vegetable stock
150g peas (fresh or frozen
   and defrosted)
100g young leaf spinach
1 small bunch basil, roughly
   chopped
2 tbsp roughly chopped
   flat-leaf parsley
salt and freshly ground
   black pepper
pangritata (see page 26), or
   Parmesan or vegetarian
   Italian-style hard cheese,
   grated, to serve

Trim the courgettes and cut into dice. Heat the olive oil in a large sauté pan over a low-medium heat, add the courgettes and thyme, and cook slowly until tender. Remove from the pan with a slotted spoon and set aside on a plate. Add the onion to the pan and cook gently until softened but not coloured. Add the garlic and cook for another minute.

Tip the rice into the pan, stir well to coat thoroughly in the oily onions and cook for a minute before adding the white wine. Cook, stirring constantly, until the wine bubbles and has evaporated, and then start to add the hot vegetable stock, one ladleful at a time. Continue to add the stock, stirring almost constantly, until the rice is tender and the sauce creamy.

Add the courgettes and peas to the pan, stir to combine and then add the spinach. Stir the risotto gently and leave the pan over a low heat for 1 minute to allow the spinach to wilt. Season well with salt and freshly ground black pepper, stir the herbs into the risotto and serve with either grated cheese or pangritata.

SPANAKOPITA

Serve this crisp filo pie either warm or at room temperature with a green and tomato salad. If Swiss chard is unavailable you could also try adding some leeks, fennel or kale to the mix.

SERVES 6

2 tbsp olive oil
2 onions, chopped
2 fat cloves garlic, crushed
6 spring onions, sliced
300g Swiss chard
325g young leaf spinach, washed and dried
3 tbsp chopped parsley
2 tbsp chopped dill
1 tsp finely grated lemon zest
200g feta, crumbled
2 tbsp grated Parmesan or vegetarian Italian-style hard cheese
50g walnuts, toasted and roughly chopped
2 medium eggs, beaten
freshly grated nutmeg
75g unsalted butter
125g filo pastry (5–6 sheets)
2 tsp sesame seeds
salt and freshly ground black pepper
30cm round baking or pie tin

Heat the olive oil in a large sauté pan, add the chopped onions and cook over a low-medium heat for about 10 minutes until soft but not coloured. Add the garlic and sliced spring onions, and continue to cook for a further minute.

Thinly slice the chard stems and roughly chop the leaves. Add the sliced stems to the pan, cook for a minute or so to soften, then add the chard leaves and spinach, and cook until they are wilted and tender, and any water released from the leaves has been cooked off.

Tip the mixture into a large bowl and leave to cool to room temperature before adding the chopped herbs, lemon zest, cheeses, walnuts and eggs. Season well with salt, freshly ground black pepper and a grating of nutmeg, and mix to combine.

Preheat the oven to 190°C/375°F/gas mark 5.

Melt the butter and brush the insides of the baking tin. Brush a sheet of filo with butter and lay it across the middle of the tin, leaving the pastry overlapping the sides of the tin. Brush another sheet of filo with butter and lay it in the tin, at an angle to the first sheet. Repeat this layering of buttered filo sheets until the bottom and sides of the tin are completely covered.

Spoon the filling into the filo-lined tin and spread level. Fold the overhanging filo pastry back over the filling and scrunch it decoratively to cover completely. Brush with more butter and scatter with the sesame seeds. Bake on the middle shelf of the preheated oven for about 40 minutes until the pastry is crisp and golden.

ASPARAGUS AND BABY LEEK TART

Look out for ready-rolled all-butter puff pastry to make this tart in moments. You can tailor the herbs to suit your tastes and what you have growing in the garden — chives would be delicious in the cream-cheese filling, and a generous flurry of dill or chervil on top wouldn't be out of place.

SERVES 6

400g asparagus
6 baby leeks
320g ready-rolled all-
　butter puff pastry
250g full-fat cream cheese
1 medium egg
1 medium egg yolk
20g Parmesan or vegetarian
　Italian-style hard cheese,
　grated
1 tsp finely grated lemon
　zest
1 tbsp chopped flat-leaf
　parsley, plus extra to serve
1 tbsp chopped tarragon,
　plus extra to serve
1 sprig thyme, leaves only
25g pine kernels
1 tbsp extra-virgin olive oil
salt and freshly ground
　black pepper

Trim the asparagus and leeks, and blanch in boiling salted water for 2 minutes. Drain through a colander and run under cold water to stop the cooking process. Cut any fatter leeks and asparagus spears in half and leave to dry on kitchen paper.

Preheat the oven to 190°C/375°F/gas mark 5 and place a solid baking sheet on the middle shelf to heat up.

Unroll the pasty onto a sheet of baking parchment on top of another baking sheet. Using the point of a sharp knife, cut a 2cm border around the pastry sheet, cutting into but not all the way through the pastry. Prick the middle of the pastry with a fork and slide the baking sheet into the oven on top of the hot sheet. Cook for 10–15 minutes until pale golden.

Meanwhile, prepare the filling. Tip the cream cheese into a bowl, add the egg, egg yolk, grated cheese, lemon zest and chopped parsley and tarragon. Season and beat until smooth and thoroughly combined.

Spread the cream cheese mixture into the pastry case and top with the leeks and asparagus. Scatter with the thyme leaves and pine kernels, and drizzle with the olive oil. Return to the oven for a further 25–30 minutes, turning the sheet around halfway through, so that the tart browns evenly.

Leave to cool slightly before scattering with extra herbs and serving with a crisp leaf salad.

SPICED TOMATO AND LENTIL RICE

This recipe is a hybrid, a melting pot of cuisines and ideas. It's part Egyptian koshari, part pilaf and part Indian tomato rice. It can be eaten on its own or as part of a greater feast. Serve with some chargrilled aubergines and roasted peppers alongside, or maybe with fried eggs and some sliced avocado. The ingredients list for this recipe may look daunting but it is mostly store-cupboard ingredients and spices.

SERVES 4–6

3 onions, sliced
4 tbsp olive oil
100g dried green lentils
2 cloves garlic, crushed
2 tsp coriander seeds
2 tsp cumin seeds
1 tsp brown or black
   mustard seeds
½ tsp crushed dried chilli
   flakes
4 whole cloves
1 cinnamon stick
a pinch saffron
1 bay leaf
200g cherry tomatoes,
   halved
150g basmati rice
1 tbsp dried barberries
   (optional, see tip)
2 tbsp coarsely chopped
   coriander
2 tbsp coarsely chopped
   flat-leaf parsley
40g pistachios, chopped
salt and freshly ground
   black pepper
lemon wedges, to serve

Start by tipping the sliced onions into a heavy-based casserole, add the olive oil and cook over a medium heat until the onions are tender and starting to caramelise at the edges.

Meanwhile, wash the lentils in a sieve under cold running water, then tip into a small saucepan, cover generously with water and cook for 10–15 minutes until just tender, but still with some bite. Drain and set aside.

Add the crushed garlic to the fried onions and continue to cook for another minute, before adding all of the spices and the bay leaf. Season well with salt and freshly ground black pepper, mix well to combine and cook for 2–3 minutes. Add the halved tomatoes, rice, barberries (if using) and drained lentils. Pour in 400ml water, stir to combine and cover with a tight-fitting lid. Reduce the heat to low and cook for a further 10–15 minutes until the rice is tender and has absorbed all of the liquid.

Remove from the heat, stir gently to break up the rice, cover with the lid again and leave to steam for 3–4 minutes. Scatter with the chopped coriander, parsley and pistachios, and serve with lemon wedges.

TIP *Barberries are small, dark red berries that have a wonderful sharp, sweet and sour flavour. They are available in the shops as dried fruits, like raisins. You could swap in dried cranberries or sultanas at a push.*

CAULIFLOWER STEAKS
WITH GARLICKY CAPER HERBY CRUMBS

A wonderfully easy and delicious way to cook cauliflower. Serve with a green salad and fries for the ultimate veggie steak dinner.

SERVES 4

2 cauliflowers
50g unsalted butter
2 tbsp olive oil
3 cloves garlic, peeled
1 large sprig thyme
3 tbsp capers, drained,
   rinsed and patted dry
3 tbsp fresh sourdough
   breadcrumbs
50g pine kernels
2 tbsp chopped flat-leaf
   parsley
1 tbsp snipped chives
salt and freshly ground
   black pepper
lemon wedges, to serve

Trim the cauliflowers and set aside any small tender leaves. Cut the cauliflowers into 2–3cm thick slices from the middle – you need 4 good slices. (Any smaller pieces can either be set aside for soup, cauliflower rice or cauliflower cheese, or they can be coated in a light batter and deep-fried.)

Melt half of the butter with the olive oil, whole garlic cloves and thyme sprig in a large frying pan over a medium heat. Season the cauliflower steaks and add to the pan – you may need to cook them in batches depending on the size of your pan and the size of the steaks. Fry the cauliflower in the butter and olive oil on one side for about 4 minutes, basting with the flavoursome butter, until the cauliflower is golden brown. Carefully turn the steaks over and cook the other side until golden. Remove from the pan and keep warm on a baking tray in a moderate oven while you cook the second batch of steaks.

Once all the steaks are cooked and keeping warm, add the reserved cauliflower leaves and fry until golden and crisp. Remove from the pan. Mash the garlic into the butter and oil, and remove the thyme sprig. Add the remaining butter to the pan with the capers, breadcrumbs and pine kernels, and cook until the breadcrumbs and pine kernels are golden and the capers are starting to crisp. Slide the pan off the heat, add the herbs and mix to combine.

Place the cauliflower steaks on plates and spoon over the garlicky caper crumbs. Sprinkle with salt and pepper and serve with a wedge of lemon for squeezing over.

PEPERONATA

This is a hard-working dish that's packed full of delicious summer flavours. It's a useful standby to have in the fridge for a simple supper. Serve with soft polenta, alongside an omelette or fried egg, or simply spooned onto toasted sourdough bread, as here.

SERVES 4–6

1 large red onion
3 cloves garlic
3 tbsp olive oil
2 red peppers
1 yellow pepper
1 orange pepper
3 large sprigs basil
400g can cherry tomatoes
1–2 tbsp sherry vinegar or
   balsamic vinegar, to taste
salt and freshly ground
   black pepper
toasted sourdough, to serve
extra-virgin olive oil, to
   serve

Peel and slice the red onion and garlic, tip into a large frying pan, add the olive oil and cook over a low heat for about 10 minutes, stirring frequently, until very soft but not coloured.

Meanwhile, quarter and deseed the peppers, and cut into 1cm wide strips, removing the white membrane as you do so. Add the peppers to the pan, season with salt and freshly ground black pepper and stir well to combine. Tuck a hearty sprig of basil amongst the peppers and cook over a low heat for about 30 minutes, stirring frequently, until the pepper strips have softened.

Add the cherry tomatoes and their juice, and continue to cook for a further 15 minutes until the tomatoes have burst and the juice has thickened slightly. Add the vinegar, taste and check the seasoning, adding a pinch more salt and pepper if needed. Remove the basil sprig from the pan and leave the peperonata to cool to room temperature.

Shred the remaining basil, add to the peperonata and mix to combine. Spoon onto toasted sourdough, drizzle with extra-virgin olive oil and serve.

TIP *When peppers are plentiful and cheap, why not make a double batch of peperonata and freeze half for another time? Add the shredded basil after defrosting and just before serving. You could also whizz the second batch in a food processor until smooth before freezing for a delicious pasta sauce.*

SWEET POTATO, SPINACH AND PANEER CURRY

Paneer is a fresh Indian cheese that doesn't melt when cooked, but holds its shape and absorbs flavour. It is widely available in larger supermarkets. If you prefer to make this curry vegan, simply swap the paneer for chickpeas.

SERVES 6

1 large onion, chopped

3 tbsp sunflower or light
   olive oil

2 fat cloves garlic, crushed

2 tsp grated ginger

2 tsp ground cumin

1 tsp ground turmeric

1 tsp chilli powder

1 tsp garam masala

3 cardamom pods, bruised

1 cinnamon stick

1 tbsp tomato purée

400g can chopped tomatoes

½–1 tsp sugar

3 medium sweet potatoes

200g paneer, diced

200g young leaf spinach

salt and freshly ground
   black pepper

Tip the chopped onion into a large saucepan, add 2 tbsp oil and cook over a low heat for 10 minutes until softened and just starting to turn golden at the edges.

Add the garlic and ginger to the pan and cook for a further minute before adding all of the spices. Stir well to combine and cook for 1 minute until the spices are wonderfully aromatic. Add the tomato purée, mix to combine and cook for another minute until lightly caramelised.

Pour the chopped tomatoes into the pan, along with 500ml water. Season well with salt, freshly ground black pepper and a good pinch of sugar, and bring to a gentle simmer. Cover the pan with a lid and cook for 30 minutes to mellow the spices and soften the onion and tomatoes.

Meanwhile, peel the sweet potatoes and cut into 2–3cm chunks. Add to the pan, cover again and cook for about 30 minutes or until the sweet potato is tender. Add 50–100ml more water if the curry is looking a little dry at this stage.

While the sweet potato is cooking, heat the remaining oil in a frying pan, add the diced paneer and cook over a medium heat until golden brown all over. Drain on kitchen paper and add to the sweet potato curry. Simmer for 5 minutes and then add the spinach. Stir gently, cover with a lid and cook for one more minute until the leaves have wilted.

Serve with basmati rice, pickles, cooling yoghurt and naan bread.

TOMATO CURRY WITH SPINACH

If you want to make this light curry more substantial, you could add some halved green beans at the same time as the cherry tomatoes. Or for the vegetarian option, add some pan-fried cubes of paneer. Either way, serve with some pilau rice, pickles and (vegan) naan breads.

SERVES 4

1 tsp fenugreek seeds
1 tsp cumin seeds
1 tsp coriander seeds
2 tbsp coconut or sunflower oil
2 onions, sliced
2 fat cloves garlic, crushed
2 tsp grated ginger
2 mild green chillies, deseeded and finely chopped
1 small bunch coriander, stalks chopped and leaves reserved
½ tsp ground turmeric
400ml can coconut milk
1½ tbsp tamarind paste
700g tomatoes, quartered
small handful curry leaves (about 12 leaves)
300g cherry tomatoes, halved
150g young leaf spinach
salt and freshly ground black pepper

TO FINISH

1 tbsp sunflower oil
1 tsp black mustard seeds
good pinch crushed dried chilli flakes

Spoon the fenugreek, cumin and coriander seeds into a small frying pan and toast over a medium heat for 1 minute until they just start to darken in colour and smell very aromatic. Grind using a pestle and mortar, and set aside.

Melt the coconut oil in a large sauté pan, add the sliced onions and cook over a low-medium heat for about 10 minutes until softened but not coloured.

Add the toasted and ground spices, crushed garlic, grated ginger, chopped chillies, chopped coriander stalks and turmeric to the onions, mix to combine and cook for a further 1-2 minutes. Pour the coconut milk, tamarind paste and 200ml water into the pan, and cook for 10 minutes to reduce slightly. Add the large quartered tomatoes and half of the curry leaves, season and bring slowly to the boil. Reduce the heat to a gentle simmer and cook for 25–30 minutes until the tomatoes have softened but still hold their shape.

Add the cherry tomatoes and continue cooking for a further 20 minutes until the sauce has reduced. Do not stir too much from this point, as you want the sauce to reduce without crushing the tomatoes.

Add the spinach to the pan, stir to just combine and cook for 1–2 minutes until wilted.

To finish, heat the sunflower oil in a small frying pan, add the mustard seeds, crushed dried chilli flakes and the remaining curry leaves, and cook over a high heat for 30 seconds to 1 minute until sizzling. Spoon over the tomato curry, scatter with the coriander leaves and serve.

BAKED GNOCCHI
WITH CHERRY TOMATOES AND CHEESE

This dish has all the hallmarks of perfect comfort food and is better for using really good-quality tinned chopped tomatoes. If wild garlic happens to be in season, a handful of leaves wilted into the warm tomato sauce would be a wonderful addition — failing that some young leaf spinach or young kale would be delicious.

SERVES 4

1 onion
2 tbsp olive oil
2 cloves garlic, crushed
½ tsp crushed dried chilli
    flakes
½ tsp dried oregano
1 rounded tablespoon sun-
    dried tomato purée
400g can chopped or
    pulped tomatoes
½–1 tsp caster sugar
    (optional)
2 sprigs basil, leaves
    chopped
500g gnocchi
12 cherry tomatoes
125g mozzarella, diced
2–3 tbsp grated cheddar
1 tbsp finely grated
    Parmesan or vegetarian
    Italian-style hard cheese
salt and freshly ground
    black pepper

Peel and slice the onion and place into a heavy-bottomed saucepan or wide sauté pan. Add the olive oil and cook over a low-medium heat for about 10 minutes, stirring frequently, until the onion has softened and is just starting to turn golden at the edges. Add the garlic, crushed dried chilli flakes and oregano, season well with salt and freshly ground black pepper, and cook for a further minute.

Add the tomato purée, mix well to combine and cook for another minute before adding the chopped tomatoes and 125ml water. Stir well, lower the heat slightly and cook the tomato sauce at a very gentle heat for a further 20 minutes until slightly thickened.

Preheat the oven to 190°C/375°F/gas mark 5.

Taste the tomato sauce, add seasoning as needed and perhaps a good pinch of sugar to balance the acidity in the tomatoes. Add the basil and spoon into an oven-proof gratin dish.

Bring a large pan of salted water to the boil, add the gnocchi and cook for 2–3 minutes until the gnocchi have all bobbed to the surface of the water. Drain well and tip the gnocchi into the tomato sauce, stirring to coat each piece. Add the cherry tomatoes and nestle the mozzarella in the gaps. Scatter with the grated cheeses and bake in the middle of the preheated oven for about 20 minutes until bubbling and the top is crisp and golden.

Serve immediately with steamed greens or a crisp green salad.

TIP *This dish can be prepared in advance and chilled until ready to cook — just add a few more minutes oven time if cooking from chilled.*

WALNUT MISO BROTH
WITH UDON NOODLES AND CRISP ROASTED PURPLE SPROUTING BROCCOLI

This walnut and seed miso paste makes more than you need for this recipe but it's not worth making it in smaller quantities, and it will keep for 2 weeks in the fridge in a sealed container. Add cubes of silken tofu to the broth for the last minute of cooking time to make this broth a more substantial meal.

SERVES 2

100g fresh shitake or
  chestnut mushrooms
½ tbsp olive oil
1 litre vegetable stock
  (made with a stock cube or
  powder)
1 tsp grated ginger
10g dried sliced shitake
  mushrooms
50g walnuts, chopped
25g pumpkin seeds, plus
  extra to garnish
25g sesame seeds, plus extra
  to garnish
75g brown rice miso paste
2 tbsp soy sauce
1 tbsp mirin
½ tsp sugar or agave syrup
200g purple sprouting
  broccoli, trimmed
2 tsp sesame oil
2 tsp sunflower oil
sea salt flakes
3 spring onions, finely
  sliced
1 tbsp rice wine vinegar
175g udon noodles
a good pinch shichimi
  togarashi

Preheat the oven to 180°C/360°F/gas mark 4.

Halve or quarter the fresh mushrooms. Heat the oil in a large saucepan, add the mushrooms and cook over a medium heat for 8–10 minutes until they are browned and tender. Pour the stock into the pan, add the grated ginger and dried mushrooms, and bring slowly to the boil. Reduce the heat to a very gentle simmer and leave to cook for about 30 minutes for the mushrooms to infuse the stock.

Meanwhile, toast the walnuts, pumpkin seeds and sesame seeds on a small baking tray in the preheated oven for 4–5 minutes until the walnuts and pumpkin seeds are crisp and the sesame seeds are golden. Leave to cool for 10 minutes and then tip into a food processor. Finely chop the nuts and seeds using the pulse setting, and then add the miso paste, 1 tbsp soy sauce, the mirin and sugar, and pulse again until combined.

Place the purple sprouting broccoli onto the baking tray, toss with the sesame and sunflower oils, season with sea salt flakes and roast for about 7-10 minutes until the stalks are tender and the tips of the broccoli are crisp.

Meanwhile, add 2 tbsp of the miso paste mixture, the sliced spring onions, remaining 1 tbsp soy sauce and the rice wine vinegar to the broth, and simmer for 5 minutes. At the same time, cook the noodles in boiling water following the pack instructions.

Drain the noodles and divide between two deep bowls. Ladle the broth on top and arrange the roasted purple sprouting broccoli on top. Scatter with extra toasted seeds, season with a little shichimi togarashi and serve with extra soy sauce if needed.

GREEN LENTIL, VEGETABLE AND ORZO STEW

A delicious one-pot dish that is even better after 24 hours. Although delicious as it is, this stew would be wonderful served with a spoonful of pumpkin seed and kale pesto (see page 127), carrot-top pesto (see page 60) or even regular pesto (using vegetarian cheese or omitting the cheese altogether for a vegan pesto).

SERVES 4

100g dried green lentils
3 banana shallots, sliced
2 tbsp olive oil
2 cloves garlic, sliced
1 leek, trimmed and sliced
   1cm thick
2 sticks celery, trimmed
   and sliced 1cm thick
1 bulb fennel, trimmed
   and sliced
1 courgette, cut into bite-
   sized pieces
800ml vegetable stock
100g orzo
150g cherry tomatoes
1 bay leaf
2 tbsp chopped flat-leaf
   parsley
1 tbsp chopped tarragon
salt and freshly ground
   black pepper
extra-virgin olive oil,
   to serve

Rinse the lentils and cook in boiling water for 12–15 minutes, or until tender. Drain and set aside.

Tip the shallots into a heavy casserole dish with the olive oil. Cook over a low-medium heat until tender and just starting to colour at the edges. Add the garlic and cook for another minute or so. Tip the sliced leek, celery, fennel and courgette into the pan, and mix to combine with the shallots and garlic.

Pour the stock into the pan and bring to a gentle simmer. Add the orzo, lentils, cherry tomatoes and bay leaf. Season well with salt and freshly ground black pepper, half-cover with a lid and cook gently for 20 minutes until the pasta is cooked and the vegetables are tender.

Add the chopped herbs and serve with a drizzle of extra-virgin olive oil and some crusty bread on the side.

SPELT 'RISOTTO'
WITH ROASTED BEETROOT, WALNUTS AND GOAT'S CHEESE

Spelt has a nutty flavour that pairs perfectly with earthy beetroot. Look out for bunches of beetroot with the leaves still attached – they will be a good indication of freshness and the leaves and stems can be sautéed to serve alongside this dish.

SERVES 4

500g bunch beetroot, with
 leaves if possible (about 5
 golf ball-sized beets)
3 cloves garlic, 1 whole and
 2 crushed
4 tbsp olive oil
1 onion, chopped
1 leek, trimmed and diced
1 sprig thyme
200g pearled spelt
200ml red wine
1 litre vegetable stock
25g unsalted butter
1 tsp balsamic vinegar
100g crumbly goat's cheese
50g walnuts, toasted
salt and freshly ground
 black pepper

Preheat the oven to 180°C/360°F/gas mark 4.

Trim the stalks from the beetroot and reserve any leaves. Place the whole, unpeeled beetroots in a small roasting tin lined with foil. Add the whole garlic clove, season with salt and freshly ground black pepper, drizzle with 1 tbsp olive oil and 2 tbsp water. Cover tightly with foil and cook on the middle shelf of the preheated oven for about 1 hour, or until tender when tested with a knife. Leave to cool and then peel and dice.

Tip the chopped onion and leek into a large saucepan, add 2 tbsp olive oil and cook over a low-medium heat for about 10 minutes, stirring frequently, until soft but not coloured. Add 1 crushed garlic clove and the thyme sprig, and cook for another 30 seconds. Add the spelt, stir to coat in the aromatic vegetables, cook for 1 minute and then pour the wine into the pan. Mix well and cook until almost all of the wine has reduced and evaporated.

Gradually add the stock to the pan, a ladleful at a time, and cook, stirring almost constantly, until the stock has been absorbed by the spelt. When you have added half of the stock, add the diced beetroot to the pan and continue to cook, adding the stock gradually until the spelt is tender and the 'risotto' thick, unctuous and rich. You may not need to add all of the stock.

Remove the thyme sprig, add the butter and season well with salt and freshly ground black pepper. Add the balsamic vinegar to sharpen and balance the richness. Cover with a lid and set aside while you sauté the beetroot leaves.

Heat 1 tbsp oil in a frying pan, add the beetroot leaves and remaining crushed garlic clove, season well and cook quickly over a medium-high heat until wilted and tender.

Spoon the risotto onto plates, top with the sautéed greens, crumble over the goat's cheese, scatter with toasted walnuts and serve.

TOMATOES AND CHICKPEAS BRAISED
WITH ONIONS, FENNEL AND HERBS

<u>VEGAN</u>

Bursting with flavour, this summery dish is one to save for when there's a good selection of colourful seasonal tomatoes available. Top with nuggets of feta or goat's cheese, or pan-fried halloumi (if not cooking a vegan version) and serve with sautéed greens and slices of chargrilled sourdough rubbed with garlic.

SERVES 4

2 small-medium onions, sliced
1 bulb fennel, sliced
4–5 tbsp extra-virgin olive oil
3 fat cloves garlic, peeled
1 red chilli, halved and deseeded
1 sprig rosemary
1 sprig thyme
1 sprig fresh sage
1 bay leaf
pared zest of ½ lemon
200g cooked chickpeas (see tip) or 400g can, drained
150ml dry white wine
400ml vegetable stock
500g mixed tomatoes (350g regular tomatoes and 150g cherry is a good mix)
salt and freshly ground black pepper

Preheat the oven to 150°C/300°F/gas mark 2.

Tip the onions and fennel into a large sauté pan. Add the olive oil and whole garlic cloves, season with salt and cook over a low-medium heat for about 10 minutes, stirring often, until the vegetables have softened and are just starting to caramelise at the edges. Add the red chilli, herbs and lemon zest, and cook for another minute or so.

Add the chickpeas, wine and stock to the pan, season, bring to the boil and simmer over a low heat for 5 minutes. Thickly slice the larger tomatoes and arrange in the pan with the whole cherry tomatoes. Season with salt and freshly ground black pepper, cover with a disc of baking parchment and cook slowly on the middle shelf of the preheated oven for 40 minutes until the tomatoes have slumped and are tender. Remove the paper and cook for a further 10 minutes.

TIP *If you have the time and inclination, soak 100g dried chickpeas overnight and cook in simmering water for about 40 minutes until tender — they are more flavoursome and cheaper than tinned.*

VEGAN SAUSAGE ROLLS

These vegan sausage rolls are filled with beans, grains, veggies and herbs, and do not contain any 'meat replacements'. Ready-made vegan puff pastry is now available in most supermarkets, either chilled or frozen.

MAKES 18

100g pearl barley, rinsed
1 tbsp ground flax seed
1 tennis ball-sized beetroot, peeled
1 large carrot, peeled
3 spring onions
1 clove garlic, crushed
400g can borlotti beans, drained and rinsed
2 tbsp Dijon mustard
2 tbsp chopped flat-leaf parsley
1 tbsp chopped sage
500g pack vegan puff pastry
plain flour, for dusting
2 tbsp dairy-free milk
2 tsp sesame seeds
salt and freshly ground black pepper

Cook the pearl barley in salted boiling water for about 15 minutes or until tender. Drain and leave to cool. While the pearl barley is cooking, whisk the ground flax seed with 3 tbsp cold water in a small bowl, and set aside for at least 20 minutes to thicken – this is called a flax egg and is used as a vegan alternative to egg.

Coarsely grate the beetroot and carrot into a large mixing bowl, and add the cooled pearl barley. Trim and slice the spring onions, then add to the mixing bowl with the crushed garlic, drained borlotti beans, Dijon mustard, chopped herbs and flax egg. Season the mixture well with salt and freshly ground black pepper, and mix together using clean hands, squeezing and pressing the borlotti beans to crush them. Taste and add more seasoning as required.

Lightly dust the work surface with flour and roll the pastry out into a neat square with a thickness of 2-3mm. Divide the filling into 3 and shape one-third into a neat sausage shape along the right-hand edge of the pastry. Brush the other side of the sausage with milk, and roll the sausage over to encase in one third of the pastry. Cut the roll from the pastry and repeat with the remaining filling and pastry.

Cut each long roll into 6 smaller sausage rolls, and arrange on a baking tray lined with baking parchment. Brush the tops with milk and chill them for 20 minutes. Meanwhile, preheat the oven to 190°C/375°F/gas mark 5.

Brush the top of the sausage rolls again with milk, cut 3 slashes into the pastry, sprinkle with sesame seeds and bake on the middle shelf of the preheated oven for about 30 minutes until the pastry is crisp and golden brown.

Serve with ketchup and mustard.

CHEESE, POTATO AND ONION PASTIES

These pasties are delicious fresh from the oven with a little salad on the side, and they also make a perfect portable treat for a picnic, long walk or lunchbox. Chilli jam is available in jars in most supermarkets, but you could also use tangy fruit chutney if that's what you prefer and have in your cupboard. Lime pickle or mango chutney would also be more than suitable substitutions.

MAKES 6

PASTRY

225g plain flour, plus extra
   for dusting
150g unsalted butter,
   chilled and diced
1 tsp poppy seeds, plus extra
   for sprinkling
¼ tsp ground turmeric
pinch cayenne pepper
3 tbsp ice-cold water
1 tsp white wine vinegar or
   cider vinegar
1 tbsp milk, for glazing
salt and freshly ground
   black pepper

FILLING

400g white potatoes, such
   as Maris Piper
2 onions
1 leek
2 tbsp olive oil
2 cloves garlic, crushed
150g tangy hard cheese
   such as cheddar or Comté,
   coarsely grated
1 tbsp snipped chives
4 tbsp chilli jam

Tip the flour into a large mixing bowl, add the chilled, diced butter, poppy seeds, turmeric and cayenne, and season with salt and freshly ground black pepper. Rub the butter into the flour using your fingers.

When the butter is almost incorporated (but still with some small flecks visible) and the mixture resembles fine sand, add the ice-cold water and vinegar. Mix to combine, first using a palette knife, adding a drop more water if needed, and then using your hands, to bring the dough together into a ball. Do not overwork or knead the dough. Flatten into a disc, wrap the dough in baking parchment and chill for a couple of hours or until firm.

Meanwhile, prepare the filling. Peel the potatoes, cut into dice and cook in boiling salted water for about 10 minutes until tender. Drain and leave to cool.

Slice the onions and leek, tip into a frying pan, add the olive oil and cook over a low-medium heat until softened but not coloured. Add the garlic and cook for another minute before adding the potatoes. Season the mixture well with salt and freshly ground black pepper and mix gently to combine. Remove from the heat and leave to cool.

When the potato mixture is cold, add the grated cheese and snipped chives.

Lightly dust the work surface with flour and divide the dough into 6 even portions. Roll the dough out, then cut into discs 16-18cm in diameter, using a plate as a guide. Lay the discs on the work surface and spoon the chilli jam

continues

into the middle of each. Divide the filling between the pastries, spooning it into a neat and compact mound in the middle of the pastry. Brush the edges of the pastry with water and fold over to encase the filling in a half moon shape. Brush the edge again with water and decoratively crimp the edge to seal.

Arrange the pasties on a parchment-lined baking tray and chill in the fridge for 20 minutes. Meanwhile, preheat the oven to 180°C/360°F/gas mark 4.

Brush the pasties with milk, sprinkle with poppy seeds and make a small steam hole in the top of each using a skewer. Bake on the middle shelf of the preheated oven for 30 minutes until the pastry is crisp and golden brown.

TIP *Cornish pasties usually have a mixture of onions, potatoes and swede, and there's no reason why you couldn't add some diced swede to the mixture in this instance too. Pasties are a great vehicle for using up leftovers and odds and ends — those leftover veggies from your Sunday roast dinner? Dice them, add some tangy cheese, and punchy pickles and you've got yourself a more than adequate pasty filling.*

ROAST ROOTS AND MUSHROOMS
WITH CARROT-TOP PESTO AND POLENTA

This recipe can be adapted a number of ways. Use whatever variety of squash you can find – butternut is always easily available, but look out for acorn or crown prince as autumn approaches. A handful of Brussels sprouts added to the mix would also be a delicious addition. The feathery leaves from the carrots make a delicious pesto – wash and dry the tender leaves before using.

ROASTED VEG

½ small butternut squash
   (or other variety of
   squash), deseeded
4 small–medium parsnips
6 carrots with leafy tops, in
   a bunch
3 tbsp olive oil
2 sprigs rosemary
2 sprigs thyme
2 cloves garlic
4 portobello mushrooms,
   trimmed
150g girolle mushrooms
   (optional)
salt and freshly ground
   black pepper

CARROT TOP PESTO

15g leafy carrot-tops,
   washed and dried
10g flat-leaf parsley leaves
1 clove garlic, crushed

continues

Preheat the oven to 190°C/375°F/gas mark 5.

Cut the squash into wedges and tip onto a large baking tray. Peel the parsnips and cut into quarters (or in half if they are skinny). Trim the stalks and leaves from the carrots and set aside (you will need 15g for the pesto). Cut the carrots in half from root to tip. Add the carrots and parsnips to the squash along with the olive oil, herbs and garlic cloves. Season well and mix to coat in the oil. Spread the veg out into a single layer and roast on the middle shelf of the preheated oven for about 30 minutes until tender and starting to turn golden at the edges.

While the vegetables are roasting prepare the carrot-top pesto. Tip the washed and dried leafy carrot tops, parsley, garlic and pistachios into the bowl of a small food processor. Season well and whizz until finely chopped. With the motor still running, add the olive oil and whizz until smooth. Taste and add more seasoning and lemon juice to taste.

Add the mushrooms to the roasting tin, mix to coat in the oil and return to the oven for about 7 minutes until tender.

Prepare the polenta according to the pack instructions, cooking until it has the texture of soft mashed potato. Add the cheese and butter, and mix to combine. Lightly stir through 3 tablespoons of the carrot-top pesto and divide between plates. Arrange the roasted vegetables on top, scatter with toasted hazelnuts and serve with extra pesto on the side.

continues

30g pistachios, roughly
  chopped
5 tbsp extra-virgin olive oil
2 tsp lemon juice, or to taste
salt and freshly ground
  black pepper

250g quick-cook polenta
4 tbsp grated Parmesan or
  vegetarian Italian-style
  hard cheese
75g diced creamy blue
  cheese (such as Cashel
  Blue) or British brie
25g unsalted butter
50g blanched hazelnuts,
  toasted

TIP *Polenta is a delicious alternative to pasta, potatoes and rice. Quick-cook polenta takes less than 10 minutes to prepare, rather than the 40 minutes it takes using the traditional method. Polenta can be bland on its own, so it needs plenty of seasoning and a good handful of cheese. If you prefer to keep it vegan, add a couple of tablespoons of vegan cream cheese, and some oat milk, and season with nutritional yeast flakes.*

LENTIL AND VEG KOFTA
IN SPICED TOMATO SAUCE

*The kofta and sauce for this dish can be prepared ahead — the kofta fried off and
the sauce made — and assembled ready to reheat. Canned lentils are a good source
of protein and a store-cupboard essential. You could also try adding some pan-
fried paneer to the mix, if you like.*

SERVES 4

KOFTAS

400g can lentils

1 courgette

2 carrots, peeled

1 green chilli, deseeded and
   finely chopped

1 small bunch (25g)
   coriander, chopped

1 fat clove garlic, crushed

1½ tsp grated ginger

50g fresh breadcrumbs

1 medium egg, beaten

¼ tsp garam masala

50g dried fine
   breadcrumbs, semolina or
   plain flour, for dusting

1—2 tbsp olive oil, for frying

salt and freshly ground
   black pepper

SPICED TOMATO SAUCE

2 tbsp olive oil

2 onions, chopped

1 fat clove garlic, crushed

continues

Drain and rinse the lentils, then leave to drain well on kitchen paper.

Coarsely grate the courgette and carrots, scoop into a clean tea towel and
squeeze well to remove excess moisture. Tip into a bowl. Add the chopped
chilli, half of the coriander (reserve the rest to garnish), the crushed garlic,
grated ginger, fresh breadcrumbs, beaten egg and garam masala, and season
well with salt and freshly ground black pepper.

Use your hands to combine the mixture thoroughly and then divide into 16
balls. Flatten slightly into thick patties and set aside.

For the sauce, heat the olive oil in a large oven-proof sauté pan, add the
chopped onions and cook over a low-medium heat for about 10 minutes
until tender but not coloured. Add the crushed garlic, ginger and spices, and
cook for a further minute or two. Add the tomato purée, mix to combine and
cook for a minute before adding the chopped tomatoes, vegetable stock and
coconut milk. Season well with salt and freshly ground black pepper and add
a good pinch of sugar. Simmer over a low heat for 30 minutes.

Preheat the oven to 180°C/360°F/gas mark 4.

Cut the cherry tomatoes in half and add to the pan. Reduce the heat and
simmer while you fry the kofta.

Heat 1 tbsp olive oil in a frying pan. Dust the kofta with either the
breadcrumbs, plain flour or semolina. Add half to the frying pan and cook

continues

1½ tsp grated ginger

1 cinnamon stick

1 tsp cumin seeds, lightly
  crushed

1 tsp coriander seeds,
  lightly crushed

½ tsp cayenne pepper

1 tbsp tomato purée

400g can chopped tomatoes

200ml vegetable stock

200ml coconut milk

1 tsp sugar

12 cherry tomatoes

150g young leaf spinach

50g toasted cashews, to
  serve

salt and freshly ground
  black pepper

until golden brown on one side before flipping over and cooking the other side. Remove from the pan while you cook the remaining kofta, adding more oil to the pan as necessary.

Stir the spinach into the tomato sauce and cook briefly until wilted. Carefully place the kofta into the sauce, slide the pan into the oven and heat for 20 minutes.

Scatter with the remaining coriander and toasted cashews and serve with warm naan bread on the side.

TIP *Vegetable kofta are found all over India and are often served with a rich sauce or gravy. Try adding some grated paneer or peas to the mixture, or perhaps some finely grated butternut squash or sweet potato in place of the carrots.*

SPECIAL FEASTS

Failsafe soufflés, fragrant curries and food for when you want to feed a crowd and pull out all the stops. Most of these dishes can be partly or fully prepared ahead of time, making them ideal party food.

SPAGHETTI
WITH SICILIAN CAULIFOWER SAUCE

VEGAN

At first glance, pasta with cauliflower sauce might seen an odd combination — however this is a vegetarian version of a classic Sicilian dish that would normally include anchovies. The capers take the place of anchovies, while raisins and saffron give the sauce an unmistakable Sicilian sweetness.

SERVES 4

pinch saffron threads
2 tbsp extra-virgin olive oil,
   plus extra to serve
1 onion, finely chopped
2 cloves garlic, crushed
1 tbsp capers, roughly
   chopped
pinch crushed dried chilli
   flakes
50g raisins
50g pine kernels, toasted
2 tablespoons sun-dried
   tomato paste
1 medium cauliflower,
   broken into florets
400g spaghetti
juice of ½ lemon
3 tablespoons chopped flat-
   leaf parsley
salt and freshly ground
   black pepper
Pangritata (see page 26),
   or grated Parmesan or
   vegetarian Italian-style
   hard cheese, to serve

Bring a large pan of salted water to the boil. Place the saffron threads in a small bowl, cover with 1 tablespoon of boiling water and set aside to soak for 5 minutes.

Heat the extra-virgin olive oil in a large sauté pan, add the chopped onion and cook over a low-medium heat until tender but not coloured. Add the crushed garlic, capers and chilli flakes, and cook for a minute more. Add the raisins, pine kernels, sun-dried tomato paste, and the saffron and its soaking water, and stir well to combine.

Meanwhile, cook the cauliflower in the boiling water for 3–4 minutes until just tender. Using a slotted spoon, scoop the cauliflower out of the boiling water and tip into the sauté pan. Season well and continue to cook for about 5 minutes, lightly mashing the cauliflower with the back of a wooden spoon.

Meanwhile, cook the spaghetti in the boiling cauliflower water following the pack instructions. Using tongs, lift the pasta from the water and tip into the sauté pan along with a ladle of pasta cooking water. Squeeze over the lemon juice, scatter with chopped parsley and mix well to combine.

Serve immediately with a drizzle of extra-virgin olive oil and plenty of pangritata or freshly grated vegetarian Italian-style hard cheese.

VIGNOLE

Make this Italian spring vegetable stew when the broad beans, peas and small violet artichokes are in season. Don't waste the pea pods but use them to make a light vegetable stock for soups (see page 101).

SERVES 4–6

6 small, tender artichokes
1 lemon, halved
2 tbsp fruity olive oil
6 spring onions, thickly
   sliced
1 fat clove garlic, sliced
6 baby courgettes, halved
   on the diagonal
200g podded broad beans
200g fresh peas
150g slender asparagus, cut
   into bite-size pieces
500ml vegetable stock
small bunch chard, roughly
   chopped
2 sprigs each basil, mint
   and parsley, leaves
   shredded
extra-virgin olive oil, to
   serve
chargrilled sourdough, to
   serve
grated Parmesan or
   vegetarian Italian-style
   hard cheese, to serve

Trim the artichokes of any woody outer leaves and stalk. Add the halved and squeezed lemon and some salt to a large pan of water, and bring to the boil. Add the artichokes and cook for 10–12 minutes – depending on size – until tender. Drain and cut into wedges, removing any remaining tough outer leaves and the furry choke in the middle of each artichoke.

Heat the olive oil in a casserole dish, add the sliced spring onions and garlic, and cook for 1 minute to soften. Add the artichokes and courgettes, and cook for another minute before adding the broad beans, peas and asparagus. Pour over the stock to just cover the vegetables, season well, bring slowly to the boil and simmer for about 10 minutes until just tender. Add the chard and cook for another 2–3 minutes until wilted and tender.

Taste, season as necessary and ladle into bowls. Scatter with the shredded herbs and drizzle with extra-virgin olive oil.

Serve with chargrilled sourdough and grated Italian hard cheese.

TWICE-BAKED SPINACH AND CHEESE SOUFFLÉS

A soufflé is often the one thing that people are wary of making – thinking that they are tricky and fraught with disaster, but not so with these. They are twice baked, and can be part prepared in advance, which takes the pressure off turning out 6 soufflés all with a perfect rise within moments of each other. Comté isn't vegetarian, but a vegetarian cheddar or Cornish Yarg work very well.

SERVES 6

60g unsalted butter

75g young leaf spinach, washed and dried

40g plain flour

pinch dry English mustard powder

good pinch cayenne pepper

225ml full-fat milk

175g cheddar, Comté or Cornish Yarg, grated

50g finely grated Parmesan or vegetarian Italian-style hard cheese

3 medium eggs, separated

250ml double cream

pinch Espelette pepper (or unsmoked paprika)r

salt and freshly ground black pepper

peppery salad leaves and good bread to serve

Preheat the oven to 180°C/360°F/gas mark 4.

Melt 10g of the butter in a medium saucepan. Add the spinach and cook over a medium heat until just wilted. Remove from the pan and roughly chop.

Place 40g of the remaining butter into the same pan and melt over a medium heat. Add the flour, mustard powder and a pinch of cayenne, stir until combined and cook for about 1 minute until the roux starts to smell toasty and biscuity. Gradually add the milk, whisking constantly until smooth. Continue to cook for a further minute or two until thickened and the flour has cooked out. Slide the pan off the heat, add 150g grated cheddar, 25g grated Parmesan or Italian-style hard cheese and the chopped greens, and mix until smooth and the cheeses have melted. Scoop into a bowl and leave to cool slightly.

Melt the remaining 10g butter and use to grease the inside of six individual pudding basins or ramekins.

Add the egg yolks to the cheesy sauce. In a clean bowl, whisk the egg whites with a pinch of salt until they hold a stiff peak. Stir one tablespoon of the egg whites into the cheese sauce to loosen the mixture, and then, using a large metal spoon, carefully fold in the remaining whites. Divide the soufflé mixture between the pudding basins and place in a roasting tin. Pour boiling water into the tin so that it comes halfway up the sides of the basins.

Cook on the middle shelf of the preheated oven for 20 minutes until golden and well risen.

Remove the soufflés from the roasting tin and leave to cool for 3–4 minutes. Run a palette knife around the edge of each soufflé and carefully turn them out of the basins and into another smaller roasting tin or onto ovenproof dishes. Leave to cool.

Turn the oven up to 190°C/375°F/gas mark 5.

Pour the cream around the soufflés, scatter with the remaining cheese and a pinch of espelette pepper, and bake for 10 minutes until golden and bubbling. Serve immediately with peppery salad leaves and good bread.

VARIATION: *If you are lucky enough to find some wild garlic then use that in place of the spinach.*

BEETROOT AND RED ONION TARTE TATIN

Earthy beetroot and sweet red onions are a wonderful pairing, and even better when cooked with crispy puff pastry. Look out for bunches of small beetroot and red onions of a similar size. If you are lucky enough to have leaves with your beetroot, simply sauté them in garlicky olive oil and serve alongside this tart.

SERVES 4–6

500g small beetroot (in a
   bunch if possible and with
   fresh leaves)
500g small red onions
15g butter
2 tbsp olive oil
2 cloves garlic, sliced
3 sprigs thyme
1 tbsp soft light brown sugar
1 tbsp balsamic vinegar
320g puff pastry
plain flour, for dusting
salt and freshly ground
   black pepper

TO SERVE

1 tbsp olive oil
2 tbsp capers, drained and
   patted dry
2 sprigs thyme
75g crumbly goat's cheese

Trim the stalks and leaves from the beetroots and set aside. Wash the beetroot and cook whole in boiling salted water for about 30 minutes, or until tender when tested with the point of a knife. Drain, leave to cool and then peel using your hands. Cut into quarters through the root.

Preheat the oven to 190°C/375°F/gas mark 5.

Peel and quarter the red onions, leaving them attached at the root. Over a medium heat, melt the butter with the olive oil in an oven-proof sauté pan with a base measurement of about 22cm. Add the onions to the pan, cut-side down, and cook for 2 minutes. Carefully flip the onions over onto the other cut-side and arrange the beetroot quarters in the gaps. Poke the garlic slices among the veggies and scatter the thyme on top.

Season the onions and beetroots with salt and freshly ground black pepper, scatter over the sugar and drizzle with the balsamic vinegar. Continue to cook for a further minute while you roll the puff pastry out on a lightly floured work surface to a thickness of 2–3mm. Cut into a disc the same size as the top of the pan, using a dinner plate as a guide.

Lay the pastry on top of the vegetables, with the pan still on the heat, and tuck the pastry in around the edges. Cut a small steam hole in the top and cook over a medium-high heat for a further minute, before transferring the pan to the preheated oven. Cook on the middle shelf for 30 minutes until the pastry is puffed and golden.

Leave the tart to rest in the tin for 2–3 minutes, and then place a serving plate on top of the pan and carefully turn the tart out onto the plate.

Heat the 1 tbsp olive oil in a small frying pan, add the capers and fry until crisp. Add the thyme and cook for a further 20 seconds. Spoon over the tarte tatin, scatter with goat's cheese and serve while still warm.

SPINACH AND RICOTTA GNUDI
IN A RICH TOMATO SAUCE

*These tender ricotta and spinach dumplings also go by the name of malfatti,
meaning 'badly made', possibly due to their rustic, hand-made appearance.
Gnudi — or malfatti — should be prepared in advance to allow them time to firm up
before poaching. If you can, make them the day before you plan on serving.*

SERVES 4

250g ricotta (the best you
  can find, preferably from
  an Italian deli)
2 shallots
50g unsalted butter
2 cloves garlic, crushed
200g spinach or mixed
  spinach and wild garlic,
  washed and dried
50g Parmesan or vegetarian
  Italian-style hard cheese,
  finely grated, plus extra
  to serve
1 medium egg, lightly
  beaten
100g plain flour
freshly grated nutmeg
2 tbsp olive oil
1 small onion, finely
  chopped
400g ripe tomatoes
pinch crushed dried chilli
  flakes
½ tsp caster sugar
salt and freshly ground
  black pepper

Tip the ricotta into a sieve set over a bowl and leave to drain for 2 hours.

Finely chop the shallots and tip into a frying pan with 25g butter. Cook over
a low-medium heat until soft but not coloured. Add 1 crushed clove garlic
and cook for a further 30 seconds. Tip the washed spinach into the pan and
stir well to coat in the butter. Continue to cook, stirring, until the spinach
has wilted into a slump. Tip the contents of the pan into a sieve and leave to
drain and cool.

When the spinach is cool enough to handle, squeeze out any moisture in
your hands. Chop the spinach mixture and add to the drained ricotta. Add
the grated hard cheese, beaten egg and half the plain flour, and season well
with salt, freshly ground black pepper and a good grating of nutmeg. Mix to
combine thoroughly.

Tip the remaining flour onto a baking sheet and, using 2 dessert spoons,
drop neat mounds of the gnudi mixture into the flour. Using your hands,
very gently turn the gnudi to coat completely in flour, and then transfer to a
clean baking sheet, making sure that the gnudi do not touch each other. Chill
the gnudi for at least 2 hours to dry out.

Heat the olive oil in a large sauté pan, add the chopped onion and cook over a
low heat for about 10 minutes until tender but not coloured. Meanwhile core
and roughly chop the tomatoes.

Add the remaining crushed garlic and a pinch of dried chilli flakes to the onions and cook for another minute. Add the chopped tomatoes and caster sugar, and season well with salt and freshly ground black pepper. Continue to cook over a low-medium heat for another 10 minutes until the tomatoes have softened and broken down. Add the remaining 25g butter and stir to combine.

Meanwhile, bring a large pan of salted water to the boil. Carefully drop the gnudi into the boiling water and cook for about 3 minutes until they bob to the surface of the water. Drain using a slotted spoon and gently stir the gnudi into the tomato sauce. Spoon into bowls and serve with extra grated Italian-style hard cheese.

SUMMER ROLLS
FILLED WITH RAINBOW VEGGIES, RICE NOODLES AND HERBS

These rolls are packed full of a rainbow of vegetables, herbs, noodles and sesame-coated tofu. The vegetable selection should be crisp and colourful, but could also include beansprouts or shredded Chinese leaf. Don't rush the assembly of these rolls – practice makes perfect and a second pair of hands is always useful!

MAKES 15–20

1 carrot
1 beetroot, golf ball-sized
50g mangetout
3 spring onions
1 small red pepper
small bunch coriander
small bunch mint
100g rice vermicelli
   noodles
100g firm tofu, drained
3 tsp sesame seeds
3 tsp cornflour
1–2 tbsp sunflower oil
20 rice-paper wrappers

DIPPING SAUCE
2 tbsp crunchy peanut
   butter
2 tbsp sriracha chilli sauce
1 tbsp soy sauce
juice of ½ lime
1–2 tsp agave syrup

Start by preparing all of the vegetables. Peel the carrot and beetroot, trim the mangetout and spring onions and deseed the pepper. Cut them all into fine matchsticks, and stack them neatly on a tray. Pick the leaves from the herbs and stack on the tray with the veggies. Cover and set aside while you prepare everything else.

Cook the rice noodles according to the pack instructions, usually by soaking in a bowl of boiling water for about 5 minutes until softened. Tip into a sieve and refresh under cold running water. Drain well and then place on a plate until needed.

Pat the tofu dry on kitchen paper and cut into neat fingers no wider than 1cm. Mix the sesame seeds and cornflour together on a plate, and roll the tofu fingers in the mixture to coat on all sides. Heat the sunflower oil in a small frying pan and fry the sesame-coated tofu in batches until crisp and golden. Remove from the pan and drain on kitchen paper.

Fill a wide bowl with warm water and dip one rice paper wrapper at a time into the water for about 10 seconds until it starts to soften. Lay the wrapper on a clean work surface and lay two coriander leaves in the middle. Arrange a neat stack of noodles on top followed by 3–4 pieces of carrot, beetroot, mangetout and spring onion. Place 2 strips red pepper and one crisp tofu piece alongside. Finally add 2 mint leaves.

Fold the bottom edge of the wrapper up and over the filling and fold the sides in to seal. Tightly roll the summer roll over to contain the filling and set the summer roll aside on a plate. Repeat with the remaining wrappers and filling.

Prepare the dipping sauce. Combine all of the ingredients in a bowl and mix until smooth, adding ½–1 tbsp water, as needed. Serve the summer rolls with the dipping sauce.

THAI GREEN SUPER GREENS CURRY

A vegan version of a much-loved Thai classic. Most Thai dishes use fish sauce — and vegetarian versions are availavle — but as this dish has plenty of chillies, turmeric, herbs and a good squeeze of fresh lime, you won't miss it. Crispy fried tofu and cashews provide protein in this vibrant curry. Serve with steamed jasmine rice and lime wedges.

SERVES 4–6

75g cashews
200g firm tofu
2 tbsp coconut oil
400ml can coconut milk
250ml vegetable stock
3 kaffir lime leaves
1 courgette
100g fine beans
8 baby sweetcorn
150g Tenderstem broccoli
6–8 spears asparagus
100g sugar snap peas or
   mangetout
small bunch Thai basil
1 spring onion, sliced
squeeze of lime juice, plus
   lime wedges to serve
salt

continues...

First make the curry paste. Combine the garlic, roughly chopped spring onions, ginger, lemongrass, chillies, sugar, cumin and turmeric in a food processor — if you have a mini attachment use that. Roughly chop the coriander stalks (save the leaves for later), and add to the food processor with the grated zest and juice of half a lime and a good pinch of salt. Whizz until combined into a paste.

Heat a large sauté pan over a medium heat, add the cashews and cook, stirring frequently, until golden. Remove from the pan and set aside. Pat the tofu dry with kitchen paper and cut into neat 1 x 3cm blocks. Heat the coconut oil in the sauté pan over a medium heat, add the tofu and cook until crisp and golden brown all over. Remove from the pan and set aside.

Add the curry paste to the pan and cook, stirring constantly, for about 2 minutes, then add the coconut milk, vegetable stock and lime leaves. Bring to the boil, reduce the heat to a gentle simmer and cook for 10–15 minutes while you prepare the vegetables.

Trim the courgette, cut it in half and then into 1cm thick slices on the diagonal. Trim the fine beans and cut them and the baby corn in half. Cut the broccoli and asparagus into bite-size pieces. Tip the tofu, cashews, courgette, beans, broccoli and asparagus into the curry sauce, and cook for about 3 minutes until the vegetables are just tender. Add the sugar snaps or mangetout and cook for a further minute.

continues...

2 cloves garlic, roughly
   chopped
2 spring onions, roughly
   chopped
2 tsp grated ginger
1 stalk lemongrass, roughly
   chopped
3 Thai green chillies,
   roughly chopped
1 tsp palm, coconut or soft
   light brown sugar
½ tsp ground cumin
small turmeric root or
   ½ tsp ground
small bunch coriander
grated zest and juice of
   ½ lime
salt

Taste and add a pinch of salt and squeeze of lime to taste. Scatter with the reserved coriander leaves, the Thai basil and sliced spring onion. Serve with steamed rice and lime wedges.

TIP *The veggie selection in this recipe is a delicate palette of greens but there's no reason why you couldn't add or swap in some red peppers, aubergines, baby carrots and add a handful of delicate spinach at the last minute. Making curry paste from scratch is always better but if you are tempted to use a ready-made curry paste check the ingredients for any non-veggie additions such as fish sauce or shrimp paste.*

GOLDEN SPICED ROOT VEG TAGINE

A beautiful golden pot of spiced stewed vegetables — this is enough to brighten up even the darkest winter day. Serve with a bowl of steaming couscous and extra harissa to add more spice if required.

SERVES 6

2 onions
3 carrots
2 sweet potatoes
1 golden beetroot (tennis-
  ball size)
½ swede
¼ butternut squash
2 tbsp olive oil
2 cloves garlic, crushed
1 green chilli, deseeded
  and sliced
1½ tsp ground cumin
1½ tsp ground coriander
½ tsp ground turmeric
½ tsp crushed dried chilli
  flakes
1 small cinnamon stick
1 bay leaf
700ml vegetable stock
400g can chickpeas,
  drained and rinsed
1 courgette
3 tbsp roughly chopped
  coriander
salt and freshly ground
  black pepper
harissa, to serve

Start by preparing all of the vegetables. Peel and slice the onions, and tip into a large casserole or deep-sided sauté pan. Peel the carrots, sweet potatoes, beetroot, swede and butternut squash, and cut them all into wedges or chunks of similar size — aim for about 3–4cm.

Add the olive oil to the onions, place the casserole over a medium heat and cook for about 5 minutes until tender and starting to turn golden at the edges. Add the crushed garlic, chilli, spices, cinnamon stick and bay leaf, and season well with salt and freshly ground black pepper. Cook for another minute until the spices smell aromatic, stirring constantly. Add the prepared vegetables and mix to coat in the spices. Pour in the stock, add the drained chickpeas and bring to a very gentle simmer. Half-cover the pan and cook low and slow for about 40 minutes until all of the vegetables are tender when tested with the point of a knife.

Trim the courgette, cut in half down the length and into 1cm thick diagonal slices. Add to the pan and continue to cook for another 5 minutes until the courgette is tender.

Scatter over the coriander and serve with a mound of steaming fluffy couscous and some harissa for each diner to add, if they like.

SALT AND PEPPER FRIED TOFU
WITH CARROTS, BEANS AND CHILLI DRESSING

Serve this hot and spicy stir-fry as part of a Chinese feast with steamed rice and a side order of Smacked Cucumber (see page 145). The tofu can be fried and the chilli dressing prepared ahead of time to make this dish dinner-party friendly.

SERVES 4

250g firm tofu
2 tbsp cornflour
1 tsp Sichuan peppercorns, crushed
1 tsp sea salt flakes, lightly crushed
200ml sunflower oil
50g raw/unroasted cashews
100ml rice vinegar
2 tbsp caster sugar
2 tbsp soy sauce
1 red chilli, sliced
1 tsp crushed dried chilli flakes
1 tsp grated ginger
1 clove garlic, crushed
1 large carrot
125g fine beans
3 spring onions, sliced

Drain the tofu well on kitchen paper and cut into 2cm cubes. Combine the cornflour, crushed Sichuan peppercorns and sea salt flakes on a small tray. Add the tofu and mix well to coat on all sides.

Heat the sunflower oil in a wok or deep-sided frying pan. The oil is hot enough when a small piece of bread sizzles and browns in about 30 seconds. Cook the tofu in the hot oil, in batches, until crisp. Drain on kitchen paper and set aside. Quickly cook the cashews in the hot oil until golden, and add to the tofu. Carefully pour off all but one tablespoon of the oil from the pan.

In a small saucepan combine the rice vinegar, caster sugar, soy sauce, sliced chilli, chilli flakes, ginger and garlic. Simmer over a medium heat for 2 minutes.

Peel the carrot and cut it into batons. Cut the fine beans in half on the diagonal. Return the wok to a medium-high heat, add the carrots and beans, and stir-fry for 1–2 minutes until tender. Add the tofu, cashews and chilli dressing, and cook for another 1–2 minutes until bubbling and hot through.

Scatter with the sliced spring onions and serve.

AUBERGINE AND PEANUT CURRY

The ingredients list for this flavour-packed dish may look long, but it consists of many store-cupboard items. Thai fish sauce is now available in vegan form — look online or in Asian supermarkets — if you can't find it, add a dash of soy sauce and a squeeze of lime juice. Serve with jasmine rice.

SERVES 4–6

1 tsp cumin seeds

1 tsp coriander seeds

3 aubergines

4 tbsp sunflower oil

3 cloves garlic, peeled

5cm thumb of ginger, peeled and roughly chopped

1 stick lemongrass, roughly chopped

1 large or 2 small red chillies, roughly chopped

½ tsp ground turmeric

1 tbsp coconut oil

400ml can coconut milk

200ml vegetable stock

2 tbsp peanut butter

4 lime leaves

1 tbsp tamarind paste

1 tbsp vegan fish sauce

1 tsp soft light brown or coconut sugar

3 ripe tomatoes, quartered

1 red pepper

4 stalks Thai basil, leaves only

2 tbsp roasted peanuts, roughly chopped

3 spring onions, sliced on the diagonal

2 tbsp coriander leaves

jasmine rice, to serve

Tip the cumin and coriander seeds into a large dry sauté pan and toast over a medium heat for 30 seconds to 1 minute until they smell aromatic. Grind the seeds using a pestle and mortar, and set aside.

Cut the aubergines in half from end to end, cut again across the middle, and then into wedges. Heat half of the sunflower oil in the sauté pan and fry half of the aubergines over a medium heat until golden brown all over. You may need to do this in smaller batches depending on the size of your pan. Remove the aubergines from the pan and cook the remaining aubergine in more oil. Remove from the pan and set aside.

Tip the garlic, ginger, lemongrass, chilli, and turmeric, along with the cumin and coriander seeds, into a food processor, and blend until combined into a paste.

Heat the coconut oil in the sauté pan, add the paste mixture and cook for one minute. Add the coconut milk, vegetable stock, peanut butter, lime leaves, tamarind paste, fish sauce and sugar, and simmer gently for 10 minutes to reduce and thicken slightly. Add the tomatoes to the pan and cook for 5 minutes until tender but still holding their shape.

Deseed the pepper, cut into 1cm wide strips and add to the pan with the aubergines and half of the Thai basil leaves. Mix gently to combine, and continue to cook for about 15 minutes until the vegetables are tender.

Serve the curry topped with the chopped peanuts, spring onions, coriander and remaining Thai basil, with bowls of jasmine rice.

VEGGIE MOUSSAKA

This veggie version of a classic Greek dish is filled with aubergines, potatoes, courgette and lentils. It can be assembled and baked straight away or prepared in advance, chilled and baked later — just add a few minutes more oven time if cooking from chilled. Serve simply with a crisp green salad and some crusty bread. Pecorino, like Parmesan, isn't vegetarian-friendly, but you can use a vegetarian hard cheese instead.

SERVES 6

2 large aubergines, trimmed
3 medium potatoes, peeled
5 tbsp olive oil
2 onions, chopped
3 cloves garlic, crushed
1½ tsp ground cinnamon
2 tsp dried oregano
good pinch cayenne
2 tbsp tomato purée
150ml white wine
400g can chopped tomatoes
1 bay leaf
1 tsp sugar
400g can lentils, drained and rinsed
1 large courgette, coarsely grated
2–3 tbsp chopped parsley
75g unsalted butter

Preheat the oven to 180°C/360°F/gas mark 4.

Slice the aubergines and potatoes into 5mm thick slices, brush with olive oil on both sides, season and arrange in a single layer on two large baking sheets. Bake in the preheated oven for about 30 minutes until tender and golden.

Meanwhile, spoon 2 tbsp olive oil into a large sauté or saucepan, add the chopped onions and garlic, and cook over a low-medium heat for about 10 minutes until soft but not coloured. Add the cinnamon, oregano, cayenne and tomato purée, mix to combine and cook for a further 2 minutes, stirring often.

Pour the white wine and chopped tomatoes into the pan, add the bay leaf and sugar, and season well with salt and freshly ground black pepper. Simmer for 10 minutes and then add the drained lentils and grated courgette. Continue to cook for a further 20–25 minutes until thickened. Add the chopped parsley and season again to taste.

Spoon half of the lentil mixture into a 20 x 30cm gratin dish and spread level. Top with half of the aubergine and potato slices and then repeat this layering.

50g plain flour
600ml milk
25g grated pecorino or
  vegetarian Italian-style
  hard cheese
1 medium egg, beaten
freshly grated nutmeg
salt and freshly ground
  black pepper

To make the topping, melt the butter in a saucepan over a medium heat, add the flour and cook for a minute, stirring constantly. Gradually add the milk, whisking until smooth and bring to the boil. Reduce the heat to a simmer and cook, stirring frequently for about 10 minutes until the sauce has thickened and is silky smooth. Remove from the heat, add the grated cheese and beaten egg, and season well. Whisk to combine. Pour the sauce on top of the moussaka in an even layer and grate over a little nutmeg. Cook on the middle shelf of the preheated oven for 35–40 minutes until golden brown and bubbling.

TIP *Traditionally, the aubergine slices for moussaka would be fried in olive oil, however, not only is this labour-intensive but aubergines are like sponges and will absorb prodigious amounts of olive oil if given half the chance. You can, if you prefer and if oven space is a premium, gently boil the potatoes in salted water until tender.*

SOUPS & STARTERS

Soups for all seasons, from hearty winter roots and vibrant spring greens to chilled Indian spiced gazpacho, as well as savoury fritters, fried snacks, dips and toasts — the perfect start to a meal or for when you want something small and savoury.

SPICED CORN CHOWDER

This warming spiced soup can easily be made vegan by swapping the milk for dairy-free milk, such as soy, nut or oat, whatever your preference. For added crunch, scatter the top of each bowl with some lightly crushed corn tortilla chips. Serve with a squeeze of lime.

SERVES 4

1 large onion, chopped
1 large or 2 small leeks, white part only, chopped
2 sticks celery, chopped
2 tbsp light olive oil
2 cloves garlic, crushed
1 tsp chipotle chilli paste
1 large white potato (about 225–250g)
250g frozen corn kernels, defrosted
500ml vegetable stock
300ml semi-skimmed milk
salt and freshly ground black pepper

SPICED CORN KERNELS

1 tbsp light olive oil
100g frozen corn kernels, defrosted
¼ tsp ground cumin
¼ tsp smoked paprika
salt and freshly ground black pepper

TO SERVE

2 tbsp coriander leaves
1 tbsp snipped chives
handful salted corn tortilla chips, lightly crushed
2 tbsp chopped jalapenos
lime wedges

Combine the chopped onion, leek and celery in a large saucepan, add the olive oil and cook over a low heat, stirring frequently for about 10 minutes until soft but not coloured. Add the crushed garlic and chipotle paste, and cook for another minute.

Peel and dice the potato, and add to the pan with the corn kernels, stock and milk. Season with salt and freshly ground black pepper, and bring slowly to the boil. Half-cover the pan with a lid, reduce the heat to a gentle simmer and cook for about 30 minutes until the potatoes are tender.

Ladle one-third of the soup into a bowl and, using a stick blender, blend the remaining soup until smooth. Return the reserved chunky soup to the pan, stir to combine, taste and add more salt and pepper as needed.

For the spiced corn kernels, heat the olive oil in a small frying pan, add the 100g corn kernels and cook over a medium heat until golden brown. Add the cumin and smoked paprika, season and cook for another 30 seconds–1 minute.

Ladle the soup into bowls, spoon over the spiced corn kernels, scatter with herbs, crushed tortilla chips and chopped jalapenos, and serve with lime wedges.

VERY ONIONY SOUP
WITH BAKED CHEESY SOURDOUGH CROUTONS

Onion soup needs long and slow cooking to bring out the best and sweetness in the onions; this is not a soup to be rushed. It's worth making double the quantity of croutons — they are incredibly moreish and it is far too easy to sneak a few before adding them to the soup. Gruyère works well for the croutons, but as it isn't a vegetarian cheese, it can be replaced with cheddar or vegetarian Emmental.

SERVES 4–6

5 white onions
2 red onions
2 leeks
3 tbsp olive oil
25g unsalted butter
2 bay leaves
1 bushy sprig thyme
2 cloves garlic, crushed
1 tbsp tomato purée
1 tbsp plain flour
1 tbsp sherry or balsamic
    vinegar
400ml medium-dry cider
    or IPA
750ml vegetable stock
pinch sugar (optional)
salt and freshly ground
    black pepper

SOURDOUGH CROUTONS

3 slices sourdough bread
2 tbsp olive oil
½ tsp garlic granules (see
    tip)
100g coarsely grated
    Cantal, Gruyère or mature
    cheddar
salt and freshly ground
    black pepper

Peel and slice all of the onions, and scoop into a large saucepan. Trim and slice the leeks, and add to the pan with the olive oil and butter. Add the bay leaves and thyme sprig, season well, cover and cook over a low heat for about 45 minutes, stirring often, until the onions are meltingly tender.

Remove the lid, add the crushed garlic, increase the heat slightly and continue to cook for a further 10 minutes until the onions start to caramelise and take on some colour. Add the tomato purée, mix well and cook for a further 3 minutes. Add the flour, mix well and cook for another 2 minutes before adding the vinegar and cider (or IPA). Mix well, then slowly add the stock and bring to the boil.

Reduce to a gentle simmer and cook for 30 minutes. Remove the herbs, then taste and add more seasoning or a pinch of sugar to taste.

Preheat the oven to 180°C/360°F/gas mark 4.

Tear or slice the bread into bite-size pieces, tip onto a baking tray and add the olive oil and garlic granules, then season with salt and freshly ground black pepper. Mix well to coat the bread in the olive oil, and cook on the middle shelf of the preheated oven for about 10 minutes until crisp and golden, stirring and turning the croutons halfway through.

Scatter the grated cheese over the croutons and return to the oven for a further minute until melted.

Ladle the soup into bowls and pile the croutons on top to serve.

TIP Garlic granules are a wonderful way to impart a good hit of flavour to cooking without running the risk of burning the garlic.

SPICED WINTER ROOTS SOUP
WITH KALE CHIPS

This is the kind of soup that makes the most of your winter veg box and can be adapted to suit your tastes and supplies. Swede is an underrated veg, but it has a delicious peppery flavour that balances with other sweeter root vegetables.

SERVES 6

1 large onion
1 leek
2 tbsp olive oil
2 carrots
2 parsnips
1 medium-sized floury
  potato
½ celeriac
½ swede
2 fat cloves garlic, crushed
1 bay leaf
1 tsp ground coriander
1 tsp ground cumin
½ tsp fennel seeds
½ tsp ground turmeric
pinch cayenne pepper
1–1.2 litres veg stock
salt and freshly ground
  black pepper

KALE CHIPS
bunch curly kale
1–2 tbsp olive oil
½ tsp garlic granules
pinch cayenne pepper

HERB OIL
2 tbsp flat-leaf parsley
  leaves
2 tbsp coriander leaves
3 tbsp extra-virgin olive oil

Dice the onion and leek, and tip into a large saucepan, add the olive oil and cook over a low-medium heat for about 10 minutes until soft but not coloured.

Meanwhile, prepare the root vegetables. Peel the carrots, parsnips, potato, celeriac and swede, and cut them into large dice. Add the crushed garlic, bay leaf and spices to the pan, and cook for a further 1–2 minutes. Tip the diced vegetables into the pan, stir to coat in the onion and spice mixture, and pour in 1 litre vegetable stock. Season well with salt and freshly ground black pepper, half-cover with a lid and bring slowly to the boil.

Reduce the heat to a gentle simmer and continue to cook for 30–40 minutes until the vegetables are tender. Remove the pan from the heat and blend until smooth using a stick blender. Add more stock if the soup is a little thick, and season to taste.

While the soup is cooking, prepare the kale chips and herb oil. Preheat the oven to 120°C/250°F/gas mark ½.

Wash the kale and thoroughly dry on a clean tea towel. Tear the leaves into pieces, removing the tough stalks and ribs as you do so. Tip the kale into a bowl, add the olive oil, garlic granules and a pinch of cayenne, and season with salt and freshly ground black pepper. Use your hands to massage the oil and seasoning into the leaves. Turn the kale onto a parchment-lined baking sheet, arrange in a single layer and bake on the middle shelf of the preheated oven for 10 minutes. Turn the kale on the tray and return to the oven for a further 10 minutes or until crisp. Leave to cool on the tray.

To make the herb oil, whizz the parsley and coriander with the extra-virgin olive oil in a mini blender or food processor until very finely chopped and the oil becomes grassy green.

Ladle the soup into bowls, drizzle with herb oil and top with kale chips.

INDIAN-SPICED GAZPACHO

A spin on the classic chilled summer soup. Traditional gazpacho is often thickened with bread soaked in water, but here I've swapped the bread with red lentils.

SERVES 6

50g split red lentils
1 tsp cumin seeds
1 tsp black mustard seeds
½ tsp coriander seeds
½ tsp fenugreek seeds
1 tbsp light olive oil
2 cloves garlic, chopped
2 tsp grated ginger
½–1 red chilli, deseeded
  and chopped, to taste
12 curry leaves
½ tsp ground turmeric
1kg ripe tomatoes
1 red pepper
½ cucumber
2 tbsp olive oil
1 tbsp tamarind paste
½–1 tsp caster sugar, to taste
salt and freshly ground
  black pepper

TO SERVE

2–3 tbsp olive oil, plus extra
  for drizzling
1 chapatti, cut into thin
  strips
handful yellow and red
  cherry tomatoes, roughly
  chopped
1 tbsp roughly chopped
  coriander
1 tbsp roughly chopped mint
2 tsp nigella seeds
lime wedges

Cook the lentils in boiling water for about 10 minutes until soft and tender, drain and set aside. Toast the cumin, mustard, coriander and fenugreek seeds in a dry frying pan until they start to smell aromatic, then remove from the pan and grind to a powder using a pestle and mortar. Heat the olive oil in the same pan and add the chopped garlic, ginger and chilli, and cook over a gentle heat until softened but not coloured. Add the ground spices, curry leaves and turmeric, and cook for a further minute.

Scoop the aromatic mixture into a blender or food processor with the cooked red lentils and set aside while you prepare the remaining ingredients.

Roughly chop the tomatoes. Deseed and roughly chop three-quarters of the red pepper (finely dice the remaining quarter for the garnish and set aside). Roughly chop the cucumber and tip all of the veggies into the blender. Add 50ml water, 2 tbsp olive oil, the tamarind paste and ½ tsp sugar. Season well with salt and freshly ground black pepper, and blend until smooth. Add a little more cold water if the soup appears too thick, and sugar if it needs a little sweetening to balance the spices.

Pour into a bowl, cover and chill for at least a couple of hours but ideally overnight to allow the flavours to develop.

The next day, pass the soup through a sieve into a jug and taste for seasoning.

Heat 2–3 tablespoons olive oil in a small pan, add the pieces of chapatti and cook until crisp and golden, then drain on kitchen paper. Pour the chilled soup into bowls and top with the cherry tomatoes and reserved diced red pepper. Scatter with the herbs, a pinch of nigella seeds and a few chapatti croutons. Drizzle with olive oil and serve immediately with lime wedges.

RIBOLLITA

This soup is a meal in itself — it's packed with flavour, full of veg and beans, and is just perfect for serving on a cold day. The base can be made a day ahead and will taste even better for it. Add the beans, bread and cavolo nero on day 2.

SERVES 6

1 large onion
2 sticks celery
1 leek
2 carrots
2 tbsp olive oil
2 fat cloves garlic, crushed
1 tbsp tomato purée
400g tin chopped tomatoes
750–850ml vegetable stock
1 bay leaf
1 sprig rosemary
400g can cannellini beans, drained and rinsed (see tip)
2 thick slices day-old sourdough bread (about 1cm thick), torn into pieces
200g cavolo nero, washed and shredded
extra-virgin olive oil, to serve
grated Parmesan or vegetarian Italian-style hard cheese, to serve

Chop the onion, celery, leek and carrots into dice, and tip into a large saucepan. Add the olive oil, and cook over a low-medium heat for about 10 minutes until softened, stirring from time to time. Add the crushed garlic and tomato purée, mix well and cook for a further minute.

Pour the chopped tomatoes into the pan, add 500ml stock, the bay leaf and rosemary sprig, season well and bring to a gentle simmer. Half-cover the pan and cook for 30 minutes to soften the tomatoes and vegetables, and then add the cannellini beans and cook for a further 20 minutes.

Add the remaining stock and bread, and cook for about 10 minutes until the bread has broken down and thickened the soup. Add the cavolo nero, and continue cooking until tender and wilted.

Serve in bowls with a good drizzle of extra-virgin olive oil and some grated Parmesan or vegetarian Italian-style hard cheese on top of each.

TIP *To use dried rather than tinned cannellini beans, simply soak 100g dried beans in a bowl of cold water overnight. The next day drain, rinse and simmer in fresh water in a large pan with a bay leaf and garlic clove for about 1 hour or until tender before using.*

CARROT AND RED LENTIL SOUP

This is served with a spoonful of harissa on top, but you could also add a swirl of yoghurt, if you like.

SERVES 4

1 large onion
1 stick celery
2 tbsp olive oil
2 fat cloves garlic, crushed
2 tsp grated ginger
½ tsp cumin seeds
½ tsp ground turmeric
pinch crushed dried
  chilli flakes
1 tbsp tomato purée
500g carrots, peeled
  and chopped
1 litre vegetable stock
small bunch coriander
100g red split lentils
1 bay leaf
salt and freshly ground
  black pepper
harissa, to serve

Dice the onion and celery, and scoop into a large saucepan. Add the olive oil, and cook over a low-medium heat for about 10 minutes until soft but not coloured, stirring from time to time.

Add the garlic, ginger, cumin seeds, turmeric, chilli flakes and tomato purée, and cook for a further minute until aromatic. Tip the chopped carrots into the pan, stir well to coat in the spiced onion mixture and pour in the stock. Chop the stalks from the coriander bunch, add to the pan with the red lentils and bay leaf, season well with salt and freshly ground black pepper and bring slowly to the boil.

Simmer for about 30 minutes until the carrots are tender and the lentils soft. Slide the pan off the heat, remove the bay leaf and blend the soup until smooth using a stick blender. Check the seasoning and add more salt and pepper if needed.

Ladle into bowls. Chop the coriander leaves and scatter over the top, then serve with a swirl of harissa.

SUPER GREEN SOUP

VEGAN

If you are using peas in the pod, don't throw the pods away as they make a delicious light vegetable stock — plan ahead and use the pea pod stock in this soup. Edible flowers or flowering chives and wild garlic would look very elegant scattered over this vibrant soup.

SERVES 4–6

1 onion
bunch spring onions
 (about 5–6)
2 tbsp fruity olive oil
1 large clove garlic, crushed
1 floury potato, peeled
 (150g peeled weight)
1 litre vegetable stock
150g broccoli florets,
 chopped
150g peas (fresh or frozen
 and defrosted)
50g young leaf spinach
75g watercress
2 tbsp chopped flat-leaf
 parsley, plus extra to serve
2 tbsp chopped mint, plus
 extra to serve
salt and freshly ground
 black pepper
crème fraiche, to serve
 (optional)
extra-virgin oil, to serve
 (optional)

Chop the onion and spring onions. Heat the olive oil in a large saucepan, add the onions and cook over a low heat for about 10 minutes until tender but not coloured. Add the garlic and cook for a further minute.

Cut the potato into large dice, add to the pan, pour in the stock and bring to the boil. Reduce the heat and simmer gently for about 15 minutes until the potato is tender when tested with the point of a knife.

Add the broccoli and peas and cook for a further minute or two to soften, and then blend the soup with a stick blender until almost smooth. Add the spinach, watercress and herbs, and blend again until smooth and bright green. Season with salt and freshly ground black pepper and ladle into bowls. Serve either with a swirl of crème fraîche or extra-virgin olive oil and a scattering of extra herbs.

TIP *To make pea pod stock, simply wash the pea pods in cold water, tip into a pan, cover with fresh water and add any other veg trimmings you might have such as tops of leeks, parsley stalks and celery trimmings and gently simmer for about 30 minutes. Strain and use the resulting stock for soups and risotto.*

CURRIED CAULIFLOWER AND COCONUT SOUP

A comforting soup for a chilly winter day, especially when served with some warm (vegan) naan breads or roti. Increase the heat of the curry powder to suit your tastes and spice tolerance, and perhaps serve with some poppadums crumbled on top for extra crunch.

SERVES 6

2 tbsp coconut oil
1 onion, chopped
1 leek, white part only, chopped
1 stick celery, chopped
1 fat clove garlic, crushed
1 tsp grated ginger
3 tsp medium curry powder (or hot if you prefer more spice)
1 cauliflower
1 small potato (about 150g), peeled and diced
400ml can coconut milk
600ml vegetable stock
1 bay leaf
1 tbsp olive oil
1 tsp cumin seeds
1 tsp black onion seeds
1 tbsp curry leaves
salt and freshly ground black pepper

Melt the coconut oil in a large saucepan, add the chopped onion, leek and celery, and cook over a low-medium heat for about 10 minutes until soft but not coloured. Add the crushed garlic, grated ginger and curry powder, stir well to combine and continue to cook for a further 2–3 minutes.

Meanwhile, trim the cauliflower, cut into quarters and reserve one-quarter and the smaller leaves for roasting. Cut the remaining three-quarters of the cauliflower into florets and add to the pan with the diced potato. Mix well to coat in the onion mixture. Add the coconut milk, vegetable stock and bay leaf, and season well with salt and freshly ground black pepper. Half-cover the pan with a lid and bring slowly to the boil, then reduce the heat to a gentle simmer and cook for about 30 minutes, or until the cauliflower is tender when tested with a knife.

While the soup is cooking, prepare the reserved cauliflower and leaves to garnish. Preheat the oven to 190°C/375°F/gas mark 5. Cut the cauliflower into small florets and tip into a small roasting tin. Toss with the olive oil, cumin and black onion seeds. Season with salt and freshly ground black pepper, and cook in the preheated oven for 10 minutes until starting to brown and crisp. Add the cauliflower leaves and curry leaves, mix to combine and return to the oven for a further 5 minutes until crisp.

Remove the bay leaf from the soup and blend until smooth. Taste and add more salt and pepper if needed. Ladle into bowls and top with the roasted cauliflower florets and leaves to serve.

SMOKY AUBERGINE
WITH TAHINI AND POMEGRANATE

<u>**VEGAN**</u>

This smoky aubergine dip or spread (known as baba ganoush) gets its wonderful flavour from the aubergines being cooked over an open flame. Although not impossible to make if you don't have a gas hob or barbecue, it won't have nearly the same depth of flavour. Serve with warmed flat breads and pan-fried halloumi or as part of a mezze spread.

SERVES 4

2 aubergines
1 clove garlic, crushed
juice of ½ lemon, or to taste
2 tbsp extra-virgin olive oil,
**   plus extra to serve**
1 tbsp tahini
2 tbsp chopped mint
2 tbsp chopped flat-leaf
**   parsley**
40g pine kernels, toasted
seeds of ½ pomegranate
salt and freshly ground
**   black pepper**

If cooking over a gas flame it's advisable to cover the surface of your hob with foil first to prevent any aubergine juices spilling and burning onto the hob — and turn on the extractor fan.

Prick the aubergines all over using a fork and place directly over a gas flame or on the barbecue. Cook for 3 minutes or so until the aubergine skin is charred and the flesh softened. Turn the aubergines and continue to cook all over until they are very soft, the insides slumped and juicy, and the skin charred all over.

Remove from the heat and leave on a plate until cool enough to handle. Carefully peel off the charred skin and scoop the flesh into the bowl of a food processor. Add the garlic, lemon juice, olive oil and tahini. Season well with salt and freshly ground black pepper, and whizz until nearly smooth.

Scoop the mixture into a bowl, add the chopped herbs and taste the baba ganoush. Add more seasoning or lemon juice as needed.

Spoon into a serving bowl, scatter with toasted pine kernels and pomegranate seeds, and serve with a drizzle of extra-virgin olive oil.

THAI SWEETCORN FRITTERS

These vegetarian fritters are perfect to serve as a starter to a Thai meal. They can be prepared and cooked in advance and heated in a moderate oven to serve.

MAKES 16–18

2 whole fresh corn cobs (or 200g frozen sweetcorn, defrosted)

75g fine beans

4 spring onions

4 lime leaves

2 tbsp chopped coriander

1 red chilli

2 tsp grated ginger

1 large clove garlic, crushed

100g rice flour

1 tsp baking powder

1 large egg (see tip)

salt

300–400ml sunflower oil, for deep-frying

sweet chilli sauce, for dipping

lime wedges, to serve

Stand the sweetcorn upright on the work surface and, using a long sharp knife, cut down the length of the cob to cut off the kernels. Tip half of the sweetcorn kernels into the bowl of a food processor and the remainder into a mixing bowl.

Trim the fine beans and cut them into small lengths, roughly the size of a pea, and add to the sweetcorn in the mixing bowl. Trim and thinly slice the spring onions, and finely shred the lime leaves. Add to the bowl along with the chopped coriander.

Chop the chilli and add to the food processor with the grated ginger, crushed garlic, rice flour and baking powder, and season well with salt. Add the egg and whiz until almost smooth. Scrape the mixture into the bowl and mix well to combine with the reserved corn and beans.

Heat the sunflower oil in a deep-sided sauté pan to a depth of about 2cm. The oil is hot enough when a small piece of bread sizzles and browns in about 30 seconds. Add the sweetcorn mixture in neat dessertspoonfuls to the hot oil, cooking 4 fritters at a time. Cook until golden brown on one side and then carefully turn using a fish slice and cook the other side.

Remove from the pan, drain well on kitchen paper and keep warm while you cook the remaining mixture in the hot oil. Serve the fritters with a bowl of sweet chilli dipping sauce and lime wedges to squeeze over.

TIP *To make these fritters vegan, swap out the egg for a flax egg. This is simply 1 tbsp ground flax seed mixed with 3 tbsp cold water and left to thicken for 10 minutes. Flax eggs are a brilliant alternative to using eggs as a binding agent in vegan cooking.*

COURGETTE, FENNEL AND BUFFALO MOZZARELLA SALAD

This is a super easy and light summer salad that's perfect as an elegant starter. Look out for buffalo mozzarella in bite-size balls or use delicate and mild goat's cheese or pan-fried halloumi, if you prefer. A handful of wild rocket or mizuna leaves on the side wouldn't go amiss either.

SERVES 4

2 courgettes
1 bulb fennel
2 x 125g buffalo mozzarella balls, drained
8–10 green olives, pitted and roughly chopped

DRESSING
finely grated zest and juice of ½ lemon
4 tbsp extra-virgin olive oil
1 tbsp shredded mint
1 tbsp chopped flat-leaf parsley
pinch crushed dried chilli flakes
salt and freshly ground black pepper

Trim the courgettes and fennel and cut into thin slices, as thin as you can get – use a vegetable peeler or Japanese mandoline if you're feeling brave.

In a bowl combine the dressing ingredients.

Combine the sliced vegetables in a bowl and spoon over half of the dressing. Mix lightly to coat and leave the vegetables to marinate for 10 minutes. Divide the courgette and fennel slices between 4 plates, tear over the mozzarella balls, scatter with chopped olives, drizzle with extra dressing and serve.

TIP *There are many variations and additions for this simple salad. If you are lucky enough to find yellow and green-skinned courgettes, use a combination of the two colours here. The herbs can be swapped around depending on what you prefer and have to hand – dill or chives would be good substitutes for the mint. And some toasted nuts or seeds would add a little extra crunch.*

CHARRED TOMATO
BRUSCHETTA

Spanish pan con tomate or Italian bruschetta are two of the most delicious ways to enjoy ripe juicy tomatoes. This simple recipe is a marriage of the two — the heat of the griddle pan softening the tomatoes and enhancing their sweetness.

SERVES 2

2 slices sourdough bread
1 clove garlic, peeled and halved
3 tbsp extra-virgin olive oil
200g cherry tomatoes
2 tbsp torn basil leaves
2 tsp balsamic or sherry vinegar
sea salt flakes and freshly ground black pepper

Heat a ridged griddle pan over a medium-high heat and toast the bread on both sides until it is nicely charred. Rub one side of the toast with one half of the garlic clove, season with sea salt flakes and drizzle with a little of the olive oil. If they are large, cut the toast slices in half.

Reduce the heat under the griddle pan and add the cherry tomatoes. Cook for about 5 minutes, turning frequently until they soften and become lightly charred and juicy.

Tip the tomatoes into a bowl. Crush the remaining garlic half and add to the tomatoes with the torn basil. Season well with salt and freshly ground black pepper. Add the remaining olive oil and mix to coat.

Spoon the tomatoes on top of the toast with any juices or oil in the bowl. Lightly crush the tomatoes with the back of the spoon and drizzle with a little balsamic vinegar.

VEGETABLE TEMPURA

Tempura is best served soon after cooking, so you will need to cook the vegetables in batches. The batter should be light and crisp, and is better for being very lightly mixed — a few lumps here and there are a good thing in this instance.

SERVES 4

1 red pepper
8 stalks Tenderstem
   broccoli
bunch spring onions
100g sugar snap peas
8 chestnut mushrooms
8 okra
8 baby corn
1 aubergine
700ml–1 litre sunflower oil,
   for deep-frying
soy sauce, for dipping

BATTER

150g plain flour
150g cornflour
300ml chilled soda water
2 medium egg yolks
salt

Pour the oil into a large wok or deep saucepan and place over a medium heat.

Deseed the pepper and cut into 2cm wide strips. Trim the Tenderstem broccoli, spring onions, sugar snaps, mushrooms, okra and baby corn, but leave them whole. Cut the aubergine into 1cm thick slices or 5–7cm long wedges.

Sift the plain flour, cornflour and a large pinch of salt into a large mixing bowl. In a jug, whisk together the soda water and egg yolks. Make a well in the middle of the dry ingredients and add the water and egg mixture. Whisk quickly to just combine the ingredients, with as little mixing as possible – a few lumps here and there are good thing with tempura batter.

Once the oil has reached 180°C/360°F on a thermometer, you can start cooking the tempura. You will need to cook the vegetables in batches so as not to overcrowd the pan and significantly lower the temperature of the oil. Tempura is best eaten soon after cooking to enjoy the crisp batter, so cook a selection of veg at the same time rather than all of one type. Dip the vegetable pieces into the batter and then carefully lower into the hot oil. Allow the vegetables to cook for a minute or so until crisp, and then turn over and cook the other side. Remove from the pan using a wire slotted spoon and drain on kitchen paper.

Repeat with the remaining vegetables, but allow the oil to come back up to temperature between batches.

Serve with soy sauce for dipping.

SALADS

*A rainbow of salads — these dishes are substantial
and delicious enough to be served as main courses.
Bright, summery vibrant tomato salads and greens with
nourishing grains are salads for all seasons.*

BLACK RICE SALAD
WITH SOY EGGS, GREENS AND AVOCADO

This is a dramatic-looking and super tasty salad. The eggs are boiled for 6–7 minutes so that the yolks remain soft, they are then marinated in aromatic soy sauce for up to 24 hours. To make this salad vegan, simply swap the eggs for marinated and fried tofu or tempeh.

SERVES 2–4

5 tbsp soy sauce

1 tbsp mirin

1 tbsp rice vinegar

1 clove garlic

½ tsp crushed dried chilli flakes

2 medium eggs, at room temperature

2 spring onions

100g black rice (see tip)

100-150g Tenderstem broccoli

75g sugar snap peas, halved

1 avocado

1 small handful Asian micro herbs (optional)

4 tsp toasted black and white sesame seeds

salt

continues

Start by cooking the soy-marinated eggs, which can be prepared up to 24 hours ahead. Pour the soy sauce, mirin, rice vinegar and 250ml water into a small saucepan. Peel the garlic, cut it in half and add to the pan with the chilli flakes. Simmer gently for 5 minutes over a low-medium heat, pour into a jug and set aside.

Rinse the pan, fill with salted water and bring to the boil. Lower the eggs into the boiling water, set the timer and cook for 6 minutes for a runny yolk and up to 7 minutes for slightly firmer. Drain and cool completely under cold running water for about 5 minutes. Carefully peel the eggs and place into the warm marinade then leave for at least 30 minutes until cold. Cover and chill for at least 2 hours, and up to 24 hours, until ready to serve.

Cut the spring onions into fine matchsticks and pop into a bowl of iced water for 1 hour until curly.

Cook the black rice in salted boiling water for about 15 minutes (or according to the pack instructions) until tender. Drain and cool under cold running water. Drain again and set aside. Refill the pan with salted water, bring to the boil and blanch the Tenderstem broccoli for 30 seconds. Add the sugar snaps and cook for a further 30 seconds. Drain and refresh under cold running water. Drain again and dry on kitchen paper.

continues

2 tbsp chopped coriander
1 tbsp mirin
1 tbsp rice vinegar
3 tbsp rapeseed oil
½ tsp grated ginger
salt and freshly ground
black pepper

Combine the dressing ingredients in a small bowl and season well with salt and freshly ground black pepper. Combine the rice, broccoli and sugar snaps in a bowl, mix with two-thirds of the dressing and spoon into a serving dish. Slice the avocado and arrange on top with the drained curly spring onions and micro herbs.

Drain the soy-marinated eggs, roll in the toasted sesame seeds to coat, cut in half and arrange on the salad. Drizzle the remaining dressing over the salad and serve.

TIP *Black rice (sometimes called Venus rice) is not to be confused with wild rice.*

CAPONATA

VEGAN

Caponata is a classic Sicilian dish that combines vegetables in a sweet and sour tomato sauce. Red pepper is not normally added to caponata but it does add another level of flavour and colour – purists can leave it out if they so choose. Caponata is best served a few hours after making to allow the flavours to mingle and marry – but it should be served at room temperature rather than chilled. Serve with or on top of toasted sourdough.

SERVES 6

2 aubergines
1 red onion
1 red pepper
2 sticks celery
5–6 tbsp olive oil
2 fat cloves garlic,
  crushed
½ tsp crushed dried
  chilli flakes
1 tbsp tomato purée
400g can chopped
  tomatoes (see tip)
2 tbsp sultanas
2 tbsp capers
1 tbsp red wine vinegar
50g pitted olives, roughly
  chopped
2 tbsp pine kernels, toasted
2 tbsp roughly chopped
  flat-leaf parsley
salt and freshly ground
  black pepper

Trim the aubergine and cut into 2–2.5cm dice. Tip into a colander, sprinkle with salt and leave to drain for 1 hour. Meanwhile prepare the remaining vegetables. Dice the red onion and red pepper, and slice the celery.

Pat the aubergine pieces dry on kitchen paper. Heat 2 tbsp olive oil in a large sauté or frying pan. Cook the aubergine in batches over a medium heat until really tender and deep golden-brown – do not over-crowd the pan or the aubergine will stew rather than brown. Remove from the pan, set aside and add more oil as needed to cook subsequent batches.

Heat another 2 tbsp oil in the same (but now empty) pan, add the onion, celery, pepper and garlic, and cook over a medium heat for about 10 minutes until really soft but not coloured. Add the chilli flakes and tomato purée, and continue to cook for a further 2–3 minutes until the vegetables are just starting to caramelise at the edges.

Add the chopped tomatoes and sultanas, season well with salt and freshly ground black pepper, reduce the heat and cook gently for about 20 minutes until reduced slightly. Return the aubergines to the pan with the capers and vinegar, and cook for a further 5 minutes.

Remove from the heat, add the olives, pine kernels and chopped parsley, and mix gently to combine.

Serve the caponata just warm or at room temperature with – or on top of – toasted sourdough bread.

TIP *You can use fresh tomatoes in place of tinned but make sure that they are ripe and packed full of flavour. Skin fresh tomatoes before using.*

GREEN FREEKEH SALAD
WITH PEAS, BEANS AND HERBS

Freekeh are the young green grains of wheat that have been dried and toasted. They are cooked and served in much the same way as rice or couscous, are a good source of fibre and protein, have a delicious nutty flavour and can be served hot as a pilaf or cold in salads.

SERVES 4–6

200g wholegrain freekeh
125g fine green beans
100g sugar snap peas
100g baby broad beans
100g peas (fresh or frozen
  and defrosted)
3 spring onions, sliced
50g cashews, toasted
50g pistachios
2 tbsp chopped flat-leaf
  parsley
2–3 tbsp chopped mint
seeds from ½ pomegranate
3 tbsp extra-virgin olive oil
1 tbsp pomegranate
  molasses
1 tbsp lemon juice
salt and freshly ground
  black pepper

Rinse the freekeh grains in a sieve under cold running water, tip into a saucepan, cover with plenty of fresh water, add a pinch of salt and bring to the boil. Reduce the heat and simmer for 25–30 minutes (or following the pack instructions) until tender. Drain through a sieve, refresh under cold running water and leave to cool.

While the freekeh is cooking, prepare the vegetables. Trim the fine beans and cut them into 3cm lengths on the diagonal. Trim and halve the sugar snaps. Refill the pan with salted water and bring to the boil. Have a large bowl of iced water nearby. Blanch the broad beans for 1 minute, remove from the pan with a slotted spoon and rinse under cold water to stop the cooking process. Peel the tough outer skins from the broad beans.

Tip the fine beans into the boiling water, cook for 1 minute, and then add the sugar snaps and peas, and cook for a further minute. Drain though a colander and refresh under cold water. Pat dry on kitchen paper before adding to the freekeh with the podded broad beans and sliced spring onions.

Roughly chop the cashews and pistachios, and add to the salad with the chopped herbs and pomegranate seeds. In a small bowl, whisk together the olive oil, pomegranate molasses and lemon juice, and season well with salt and freshly ground black pepper. Pour the dressing into the salad and mix well to combine. Leave the salad for 30 minutes before serving to allow all of the flavours to combine.

VARIATIONS: *There is quite a selection of veg and herbs in this salad, but use whatever you prefer or is in season – just keep the ratio of veg to grains the same. A couple of pickled green chillies, roughly chopped, are a wonderful addition for a hit of flavour and some crumbled feta adds an extra salty note.*

GADO GADO

This Indonesian salad is rainbow of crisp vegetables with a spicy peanut dressing. The selection of vegetables is (and should be) varied and colourful, but use whatever you have, prefer and is in season or growing in your garden.

SERVES 4

3 medium eggs, at room
   temperature
200g new potatoes
100g fine beans
200g firm tofu, drained and
   patted dry
1 tbsp sunflower or sesame
   oil
1 large carrot
½ cucumber or 3 baby
   cucumbers
3 spring onions
1 bunch radishes
handful beansprouts
¼ Chinese leaf, shredded
handful coriander leaves
2 tbsp crispy fried onions
2 tbsp roasted peanuts
lime wedges, to serve

DRESSING

2 tbsp peanut butter
2 tbsp soy sauce, plus extra
   to taste
1 tbsp tamarind paste
juice of ½ lime, plus extra
   to taste
1 tbsp soft light brown or
   coconut sugar
1 clove garlic, crushed
1 red chilli, roughly
   chopped
150ml coconut milk

Start by hard-boiling the eggs – gently lower the room-temperature eggs into boiling water and cook for 8 minutes. Drain, cool under cold running water for at least 5 minutes and peel.

Cook the new potatoes in salted boiling water until tender. Drain, leave to cool, and then cut in half or quarters depending on size.

Rinse the saucepan, refill with boiling water and cook the fine beans for 1 minute, then drain and refresh.

Cut the tofu into bite-size pieces. Heat the oil in a frying pan over a medium heat and fry the tofu until crisp. Drain on kitchen paper and set aside.

Cut the carrot into matchsticks and slice the cucumber, spring onions and radishes.

To make the dressing, tip all of the ingredients into a mini food processor and whizz until combined. Spoon the dressing into a small pan and cook over a low-medium heat until reduced slightly. Taste and add a little more soy sauce or lime juice to taste. Spoon the dressing into a bowl and place on a serving plate.

Arrange the vegetables, quartered eggs and tofu around the dressing. Scatter with coriander leaves, fried onions and peanuts, and serve with extra lime wedges on the side.

TOMATO AND CHARGRILLED PEACH SALAD
WITH BUFFALO MOZZARELLA AND BASIL–OIL DRESSING

The success of this salad really does depend on the ripeness and flavour of the raw ingredients used. The peaches must be ripe and juicy, as should the tomatoes. Chargrilling the peaches really exaggerates their sweetness, which is a wonderful contrast to the cooling creaminess of the buffalo mozzarella. If you happen to have the BBQ lit for something else then by all means use that to cook the peaches.

SERVES 4

4 ripe peaches
1–2 tbsp olive oil
good handful wild rocket
200g mixed tomatoes,
  sliced
2 x 125g balls buffalo
  mozzarella
handful purple basil
freshly ground black
  pepper

BASIL–OIL DRESSING

50g basil leaves
1 clove garlic
2 tbsp flat-leaf parsley
dash lemon juice
100ml extra-virgin olive oil
salt and freshly ground
  black pepper

Start by making the dressing. Tip the basil into the bowl of a mini processor and whizz until finely chopped. Add the garlic and parsley, and whizz again to combine. Add the lemon juice and half of the oil, season well with salt and freshly ground black pepper and blend until almost smooth. Add the remaining oil and whizz once more. Leave to one side for 30 minutes for all of the flavours to mingle, after which time taste and add more salt and pepper as needed. You can strain the dressing though a fine sieve if you would rather a smooth vibrant green dressing.

Heat a ridged griddle pan over a medium-high heat. Cut the peaches in half, remove the stones and cut the fruit into wedges. Brush the cut sides of the peaches with a little olive oil and cook on the hot griddle pan until nicely charred.

Arrange the rocket on each plate and top with peaches and sliced tomatoes. Using your hands, tear the mozzarella balls in half and divide between the plates. Spoon the dressing over each salad, scatter with basil and finish with freshly ground black pepper.

GARLICKY GREEN BEAN SALAD
WITH MINT AND DILL

This is a salad to make in the summer months when peas and beans are at their best. Ideally use fresh peas in the pod. The weight given is for podded peas, but don't waste the pods — they can be used to make a delicious and light stock for summer soups or risotto (see page 101).

SERVES 4–6

200g fine beans
125g sugar snap peas or
   mangetout
150g runner beans
100g fresh peas (podded
   weight)
juice and zest of ½ lemon
1 clove garlic, crushed
1 tsp Dijon mustard
3 tbsp extra-virgin olive oil
2 tbsp roughly chopped dill
2 tbsp roughly chopped
   mint
1 tsp poppy seeds
25g whole almonds, roughly
   chopped or sliced
salt and freshly ground
   black pepper

Trim the fine beans, sugar snaps and runner beans. Cut the sugar snaps in half and the runner beans into thin diagonal slices.

Bring a large saucepan of salted water to the boil. Add the fine beans and cook for 1 minute. Add the sugar snaps, runner beans and peas, and cook for another minute. Drain through a colander and cool under cold running water to completely stop the cooking process and to preserve the bright green colour of the vegetables. Drain well and leave to dry on kitchen paper while you prepare the dressing.

Pour the lemon juice into a small bowl, add the crushed garlic and Dijon mustard, and mix to combine. Whisk in the olive oil, and season well with salt and freshly ground black pepper. Tip the beans and peas into a large bowl, pour over the dressing, add the lemon zest, chopped herbs, poppy seeds and chopped almonds and mix to combine thoroughly. Leave the beans to absorb the dressing for 15 minutes before serving.

CELERY SALAD
WITH APPLES AND KOHLRABI

VEGAN

A crisp, coleslaw-style salad that is quick to prepare and perfect to serve with chargrilled veggies or rich moussaka. If you're not following a vegan diet, try adding 1–2 tablespoons natural yoghurt or buttermilk for a light, creamy dressing.

SERVES 6

3 large celery sticks, including the tender inner leaves

1 Braeburn or other crisp apple

½ small celeriac (about 200g)

1 small kohlrabi (tennis ball size)

75g walnuts or pecans, toasted

2 tbsp roughly chopped flat-leaf parsley

1 tbsp lemon juice or cider vinegar

2–3 tbsp extra-virgin olive oil or rapeseed oil

good handful small watercress leaves

salt and freshly ground black pepper

Cut the celery into matchsticks, roughly chop the leaves and place in a large bowl. Core the apple, cut into matchsticks and add to the celery.

Peel the celeriac and kohlrabi, and cut into similar size pieces as the celery and apple. Add to the bowl. Roughly chop the nuts, add to the vegetables with the chopped parsley, lemon juice and olive oil, and season well with salt and freshly ground black pepper. Mix well to combine and leave for 15–20 minutes for the flavours to mingle, before gently stirring through the watercress and spooning into a dish to serve.

TIP *Kohlrabi is a curious-looking vegetable. A pale green orb with long stalks and chard-like leaves, it has a delicious crisp apple or radish texture and is wonderful in raw salads. The leaves can be sautéed with olive oil and garlic in much the same way as kale or chard. If you can't find kohlrabi, try swapping in fennel.*

HOT AND SOUR CARROT AND CHICKPEA SALAD
WITH PRESERVED LEMON AND TOASTED SEEDS

<u>VEGAN</u>

A north African-inspired salad that packs a punch with flavour from herbs, spices and harissa. Preserved lemons, harissa, pomegranate molasses and sumac are all available in large supermarkets, and are invaluable store-cupboard items, vital for warming tagines and couscous.

SERVES 4–6

500g carrots (about 5
  medium carrots)
4 spring onions
1 green chilli, deseeded
1 small preserved lemon,
  skin only
1 small bunch dill, roughly
  chopped
1 small bunch coriander,
  roughly chopped
4 tbsp fruity olive oil
1 tbsp lemon juice, or to
  taste
2 tsp rose harissa paste, or
  to taste
2 tsp pomegranate molasses
  or honey
½ tsp sumac
½ tsp ground cumin
½ tsp ground coriander
¼ tsp cayenne pepper
200g tinned chickpeas,
  drained
3 tbsp mixed seeds
  (pumpkin, sunflower,
  sesame, linseed)
salt and freshly ground
  black pepper
flat breads, to serve

Peel the carrots and cut into fine matchsticks, either by hand or by using a food processor, and place in a large mixing bowl. Trim and slice the spring onions and add to the bowl. Slice the green chilli and skin of the preserved lemon (you will not need to use the flesh) and add to the bowl along with the chopped herbs.

To make the dressing, combine 3 tbsp olive oil, the lemon juice, harissa, pomegranate molasses and sumac in a bowl, and season well. Taste and add more harissa for extra kick or lemon juice for extra zip. Spoon the dressing in with the carrots, stir to combine and leave the salad to sit for 10 minutes to allow the flavours to mingle.

Heat the remaining tablespoon of olive oil in a frying pan, add the cumin, coriander, cayenne and chickpeas, and cook over a medium heat for 2–3 minutes until the chickpeas start to crisp. Add the mixed seeds, cook for another minute and tip into the carrot salad. Stir to combine and serve at room temperature with warm flat breads.

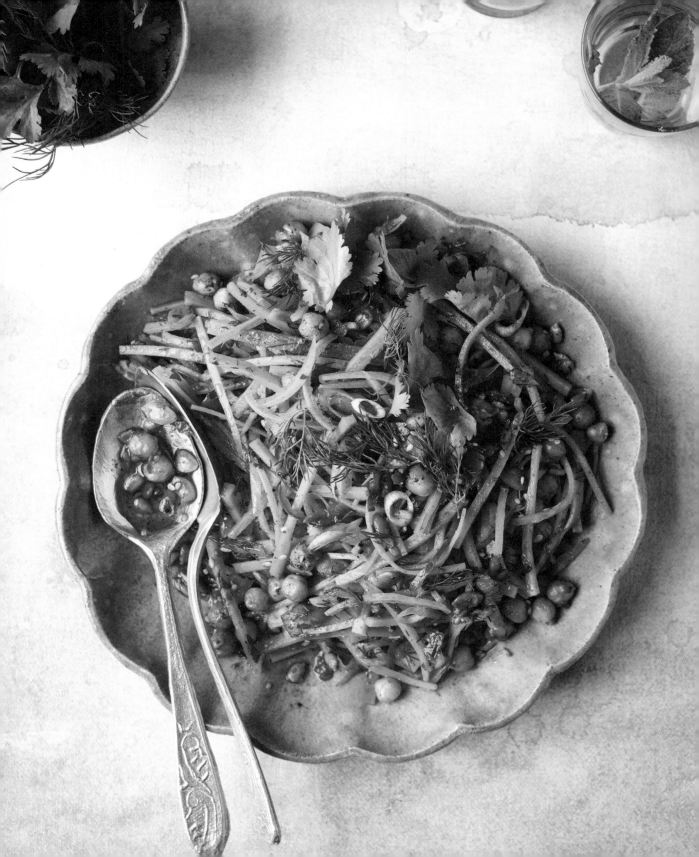

MIXED GRAINS
WITH ROASTED BUTTERNUT SQUASH, CAVOLO NERO AND WALNUTS

Look out for mixed or rainbow quinoa — a combination of red, brown and white grains. Omit the cheese if you prefer this salad to be vegan, and use agave in place of honey in the dressing.

SERVES 4–6

500g butternut squash
   (½ medium butternut
   squash)
1–2 tbsp olive oil
75g walnuts
75g bulgur wheat
75g rainbow quinoa
100g cavolo nero
2 sticks celery
4 spring onions
75g dried cranberries
2 tbsp roughly chopped
   mint
2 tbsp roughly chopped
   flat-leaf parsley
100g halloumi or feta
   (optional)
salt and freshly ground
   black pepper

DRESSING

3 tbsp extra-virgin olive oil
1 tbsp white wine vinegar or
   lemon juice
2 tsp Dijon mustard
½ clove garlic, crushed
2 tsp agave or honey
salt and freshly ground
   black pepper

Preheat the oven to 190°C/375°F/gas mark 5.

Deseed the butternut squash, cut into 1–2cm thick wedges and tip into a roasting tin in a single layer. Season with salt and freshly ground black pepper, and drizzle with the olive oil. Mix to coat, then roast for about 30 minutes or until tender and starting to caramelise at the edges. While the oven is on, toast the walnuts on another tray for 2–3 minutes until crisp. Leave the squash and nuts to cool while you prepare the remaining salad ingredients.

Rinse the bulgur wheat in a sieve under cold running water and cook in twice the volume of lightly salted water for 3 minutes. Turn the heat off and leave to soak for a further 5 minutes. Drain and cool.

Rinse the quinoa in a sieve and again cook in twice the volume of lightly salted water for 10–12 minutes (or according to the pack instructions) until tender. Drain, run under cold water and leave to dry thoroughly.

Remove the tough rib from the cavolo nero, cut the leaves into 1cm wide ribbons and scoop into a large bowl. Trim and slice the celery and spring onions, and add to the bowl with the dried cranberries and chopped herbs.

Roughly chop the toasted walnuts and cut the roasted squash into large dice — you can leave it in whole wedges if you prefer a more chunky salad. Add the drained bulgur and quinoa, and gently mix to combine.

Whisk the dressing ingredients together in a small bowl or jug, season with salt and freshly ground black pepper, and pour over the salad. Mix again to combine and set aside for 10 minutes for the grains to absorb the flavours. Scoop the salad onto a large platter, grate the halloumi (or crumble the feta) over the top, if using, and serve.

ROAST HERITAGE CARROT, FENNEL AND FARRO SALAD

Farro is a delicious nutty grain that is perfect for salads and hearty stews. If farro is not available you can use pearl barley or spelt instead. This salad benefits from being made a couple of hours ahead of serving to allow the flavours to mingle.

SERVES 4–6

150g farro or pearl barley

600g fresh young carrots or Chantenay

2 small bulbs fennel

2 fat cloves garlic

2 tbsp olive oil

4–5 pitted medjool dates, roughly chopped, or 75g dried sour cherries

50g whole almonds, roughly chopped

2 tbsp flat-leaf parsley leaves, very roughly chopped

2 tbsp extra-virgin olive oil

1 tbsp white wine vinegar

1 tsp maple or date syrup

100g crumbly goat's cheese

PUMPKIN SEED AND KALE PESTO

50g pumpkin seeds, toasted

50g tender kale leaves, torn, washed and dried

25g flat-leaf parsley leaves

25g basil leaves

1 fat clove garlic

4 tbsp extra-virgin olive oil

1–2 tbsp lemon juice, to taste

salt and freshly ground black pepper

Preheat the oven to 190°C/375°F/gas mark 5.

Rinse the farro in a sieve under cold running water and cook in boiling salted water for about 10 minutes (or according to the pack instruction) until tender. Drain and refresh under cold running water, then leave to drain thoroughly.

Cut the carrots into thick slices on the diagonal and the fennel into 1cm thick slices through the root. Tip the veg onto a baking tray, add the whole, unpeeled garlic cloves, season, drizzle with the olive oil and mix to coat. Cook on the middle shelf of the preheated oven for about 30 minutes or until tender and starting to caramelise at the edges.

Prepare the pesto while the veg are roasting. Toast the pumpkin seeds on a small tray in the oven for 5 minutes until crisp. Leave to cool and then tip into the food processor bowl with the torn kale leaves, flat-leaf parsley, basil and garlic. Whizz until finely chopped. Add the extra-virgin olive oil, 1 tbsp lemon juice and season well with salt and freshly ground black pepper. Whizz again until almost smooth, taste and add more lemon juice or seasoning as needed. Spoon into a tub or bowl, cover and chill until needed.

Combine the farro, carrots and fennel in a large bowl. Add the dates, almonds and flat-leaf parsley, and mix to combine. In a small bowl, combine the extra-virgin olive oil, vinegar and maple or date syrup. Squeeze the roasted garlic from its skin into the dressing, season well and whisk to combine. Pour the dressing over the salad, mix well and leave for 30 minutes to allow the flavours to mingle.

Spoon the salad onto a serving dish, dot teaspoons of the pesto over the top (you will need about 3 tbsp altogether), crumble over the goat's cheese and serve.

HEIRLOOM TOMATO AND AVOCADO SALAD
WITH CUCUMBER AND RADISHES

Flavoursome and beautiful, heirloom tomatoes are now widely available from early summer through to autumn. The various shapes, sizes and colours make for a stunning, jewel-like salad. Look out for small or mini cucumbers and radishes in assorted colours to make this salad even prettier than it already is.

SERVES 6

1kg heirloom tomatoes in
  a mixture of shapes, sizes
  and colours
3 mini cucumbers or ¼
  regular cucumber
8–10 radishes
1 avocado
1 small clove garlic, crushed
juice of ½ lemon
4 tbsp extra-virgin olive oil
1 tsp pomegranate
  molasses, agave or maple
  syrup
1 rounded tbsp chopped dill
1 rounded tbsp chopped
  coriander
pinch sumac
salt and freshly ground
  black pepper

Cut the larger tomatoes into wedges or slices and the smaller ones into halves or quarters, and combine on a large serving dish.

Cut the cucumbers in half and then into 5mm thick slices on the diagonal. Add to the tomatoes. Trim and thinly slice the radishes. Peel and stone the avocado, and cut into slices. Add the radishes and avocado to the tomatoes.

Combine the crushed garlic, lemon juice, extra-virgin olive oil and pomegranate molasses (or agave or maple syrup) in a small jug or bowl, and season well with salt and freshly ground black pepper. Pour the dressing over the salad, add the dill and coriander, and mix gently to combine.

Scatter with a pinch of sumac and leave to sit for 15 minutes before serving to allow the dressing to flavour the tomatoes.

FATTOUSH WITH CRISP SPICED CHICKPEAS

Save this salad for the height of summer when tomatoes are at their best and baby cucumbers are easy to come by. You can, of course, use ½ regular cucumber, but remove the seeds with a teaspoon to prevent it becoming watery.

SERVES 4

200g drained tinned
  chickpeas
2 tbsp olive oil
½ tsp ground cumin
½ tsp ground coriander
¼ tsp cayenne pepper, plus
  a pinch
2 pitta breads
a good pinch dried oregano
a good pinch garlic granules
4 large ripe tomatoes
120g cherry or baby plum
  tomatoes
4 baby cucumbers
3–4 spring onions
100g radishes
2 baby gem lettuces or ruby
  baby gem
3 tbsp roughly chopped flat-
  leaf parsley
2 tbsp roughly chopped mint
a pinch sumac
salt and freshly ground
  black pepper

DRESSING
1 clove garlic
juice of ½ lemon
½ tbsp pomegranate
  molasses
4 tbsp extra-virgin olive oil
½ tbsp white wine vinegar
salt and freshly ground
  black pepper

Preheat the oven to 180°C/360°F/gas mark 4.

Tip the chickpeas into a small roasting tin, add 1 tablespoon olive oil, the ground cumin, coriander and the ¼ tsp cayenne, and season well. Mix to coat the chickpeas in the spices, and then roast in the preheated oven for about 20 minutes until golden and crisp.

While the chickpeas are cooking, tear the pitta breads into bite-size pieces. Place them on another baking sheet and add the dried oregano, garlic granules, the pinch of cayenne and 1 tbsp olive oil, and season well with salt and freshly ground black pepper. Mix well to combine and toast in the oven for 5–6 minutes until crisp and golden. Remove from the oven and leave the chickpeas and pittas to cool.

Cut the large tomatoes into chunks and the cherry tomatoes in half, and tip into a large bowl. Halve the cucumbers and cut into slices on the diagonal, then add to the tomatoes. Trim and slice the spring onions and radishes, and add to the tomatoes. Roughly slice or quarter the baby gem and add to the salad with the chopped herbs.

Combine the dressing ingredients in a bowl and mix with a fork to combine. Pour the dressing into the salad, add the toasted chickpeas and pitta pieces, and mix to combine.

Let the salad sit for 3–4 minutes for the dressing to permeate the salad and toasted pitta, and then sprinkle with a pinch of sumac and serve.

VARIATION *Try adding a handful of pomegranate seeds and perhaps serving with some crumbled feta alongside.*

SIDES

Garlicky potato and tomato focaccia, creamy gratins, roasted spuds, and slow-cooked confit tomatoes — flavoursome dishes to serve alongside the main event.

CARROT, COURGETTE AND GRUYÈRE LOAF

This wheat-free loaf is delicious served spread with butter and with a bowl of soup. Gruyère isn't a vegetarian cheese, but it can be replaced with vegetarian Emmental or cheddar.

SERVES 6

100g coarsely grated carrot
75g coarsely grated
  courgette
250g spelt flour
2 tsp baking powder
½ tsp paprika
½ tsp garlic granules
3 spring onions
100g grated Gruyère,
  vegetarian Emmental or
  mature Cheddar
2 tsp nigella or black cumin
  seeds
3 large eggs, lightly beaten
100g fruity olive oil
salt and freshly ground
  black pepper

Preheat the oven to 180°C/360°F/gas mark 4 and line a 900g loaf tin with a strip of buttered baking parchment.

Sit the grated carrot and courgette on a plate lined with kitchen paper to remove any excess moisture and set aside for 10 minutes.

Sift the flour, baking powder, paprika and garlic granules into a large bowl and season well with salt and freshly ground black pepper. Trim and finely chop the spring onions.

Make a well in the middle of the dry ingredients, and add the spring onions, carrot, courgette and all but 1 tablespoon of the grated cheese. Add 1 teaspoon of the nigella seeds, the beaten eggs and olive oil, and mix well to combine thoroughly.

Spoon the batter into the prepared loaf tin; it will be quite stiff, so use the back of the spoon to level the top of the loaf. Sprinkle with the remaining cheese and nigella seeds, and bake on the middle shelf of the preheated oven for 40 minutes until risen and golden brown. A skewer inserted into the middle of the loaf should come out clean.

Leave the loaf to cool in the tin for 10 minutes and then turn out onto a wire rack. Serve the loaf warm or at room temperature with butter and a bowl of soup.

CORN ON THE COB
WITH SPICED BUTTER

You can simply pop the corn on the barbecue in its husk and leave to cook for about 10-15 minutes, turning frequently until the husk is blackened and the kernels inside will be tender and lightly charred. All you then need is a good pinch of sea salt flakes and some butter to melt over the corn. To take corn to another level serve it with this spiced butter, which is seasoned with smoked paprika. You could use chipotle or harissa paste if you prefer — just go easy though, as they have more of a kick than smoked paprika, which has a milder, warming heat.

SERVES 4

4 ears of corn, still in the green husk if possible (see tip)

100g butter, at room temperature

2 tsp smoked paprika

2 cloves garlic, crushed

sea salt flakes and freshly ground black pepper

2 tbsp grated halloumi, crumbled feta or ricotta salata, to serve (optional)

2 tbsp roughly chopped coriander, to serve (optional)

lime wedges, to serve

Preheat the barbecue or a ridged griddle pan depending on whether you are cooking outdoors or indoors.

Place the corn on the hot barbecue or ridged griddle pan (if on the barbecue you can leave it in the husks; if cooking inside on the griddle pan, you'll need to remove the leaves). Turning frequently, cook the corn on all sides for about 10 minutes until the kernels are tender and starting to char in places.

While the corn is cooking, prepare the butter. In a bowl, combine the softened butter, smoked paprika, crushed garlic and a good seasoning of sea salt flakes and freshly ground black pepper.

When the corn is cooked, remove from the heat and brush liberally with the seasoned butter. Scatter with grated halloumi, feta or ricotta salata and chopped coriander, if using. Serve immediately with plenty of cloth napkins and lime wedges for squeezing over.

TIP *In the height of summer look out for ears of corn still wrapped in their green husks — this a good sign that the corn is freshly cut and the kernels inside should be firm and juicy.*

HASSELBACK POTATOES – SWEET AND NOT SO SWEET

VEGAN

These crispy yet tender potatoes not only look very beautiful but are flavoured with a delicious selection of woody herbs and a hint of smoked paprika, elevating Sunday lunch to dizzy heights. Cutting potatoes into wafer-thin slices isn't the easiest task but follow the neat trick here using a wooden skewer to avoid any chunky pieces or cut fingers. This recipe can easily be doubled to feed a crowd.

SERVES 4–6

3 medium-sized sweet
   potatoes
3 medium-sized potatoes,
   such as Maris Piper
1 sprig rosemary
4 bay leaves
2 sprigs fresh sage
4–6 cloves garlic
3 tbsp olive oil
¼ tsp smoked paprika
salt and freshly ground
   black pepper

Preheat the oven to 200°C/400°F/gas mark 6.

Wash the potatoes. Lay one potato on the work surface and push a wooden skewer into the potato, along the length and 1cm up from the bottom. Using a good sharp knife, cut the potato vertically into very thin slices, cutting down to but not through the wooden skewer – this acts as a marker, but also holds the potato together as you are cutting. Carefully remove the skewer and repeat with all of the potatoes.

Arrange the potatoes snugly in an oven-proof dish and tuck the herbs in amongst them. Lightly crush the whole garlic cloves with the flat side of a knife and scatter into the gaps.

Drizzle the olive oil over the potatoes and season well with salt, freshly ground black pepper and smoked paprika. Cook on the middle shelf of the preheated oven for about 30 minutes and then baste with the herby olive oil. Continue to cook for a further 30–40 minutes until the potatoes are crisp, golden and tender.

MUHAMMARA

This red pepper dip originates in Aleppo, Syria, and is served as part of a mezze selection. It can be thickened with breadcrumbs or toasted walnuts, as in this recipe, which means that this is not only vegan but gluten-free, too. Add a little extra smoked paprika if you want a little more spice.

SERVES 4–6

2 red peppers
2 ripe tomatoes
1 red chilli
1 small red onion, peeled
  and halved through the
  root
3 tbsp extra-virgin olive oil,
  plus extra to serve
2 large cloves garlic
100g walnuts
1 tbsp pomegranate
  molasses
½ tsp ground cumin
salt and freshly ground
  black pepper

Preheat the oven to 200°C/400°F/gas mark 6.

Place the whole peppers, tomatoes, red chilli and red onion, cut-side down, in a small roasting tin. Drizzle with 1 tbsp olive oil and cook on the middle shelf of the preheated oven for 20 minutes. Add the whole, unpeeled garlic cloves to the tin, and continue to cook for another 10 minutes. By this time the vegetables should be nicely charred and the skins of the peppers, tomatoes and chilli blistered.

Remove the veg from the oven, turn the heat down to 180°C/360°F/gas mark 4, and toast the walnuts on another baking tray for 5 minutes.

When the vegetables have cooled, remove the skin and seeds from the peppers and chilli, and tip the flesh into a food processor. Add the charred tomatoes and red onion, along with any pan juices. Add the toasted walnuts, remaining extra-virgin olive oil, pomegranate molasses and ground cumin, and season well with salt and freshly ground black pepper. Use the pulse button on the mixer and blend until the ingredients are combined and almost smooth, but still with some texture.

Spoon the muhammara into a bowl and add more salt and pepper as needed. Cover and chill for 2 hours to allow all of the flavours to mingle, before serving drizzled with extra-virgin olive oil.

ZA'ATAR-ROASTED SWEET POTATO FRIES

Za'atar is a Middle Eastern spice blend containing sesame, cumin, sumac and a dried herb (usually thyme, oregano or marjoram). It adds a wonderful savoury flavour to simple dishes such as eggs, flatbreads and potatoes. It is now widely available in supermarkets or easy to make yourself at home.

SERVES 4

4 medium-large sweet
  potatoes
2 tbsp olive oil
2 tsp za'atar
salt and freshly ground
  black pepper
lime wedges, to serve

YOGHURT DIP

5 tbsp natural yoghurt
2 tbsp chopped coriander
pinch cayenne pepper or
  smoked paprika
salt and freshly ground
  black pepper

Preheat the oven to 190°C/375°F/gas mark 5.

Peel the sweet potatoes and cut each potato into fat finger-width chips or wedges. Tip into a large bowl, add the olive oil and za'atar, and season well with salt and freshly ground black pepper. Mix well to coat, and then arrange the fries in a single layer on a large baking tray. Don't overcrowd the tray – to ensure the fries crisp up, they need a little space between them.

Cook on the middle shelf of the preheated oven for about 25 minutes, and then turn the fries over. Return to the oven and continue to cook for a further 20–25 minutes until the fries are crisp and golden on the outside and tender within.

Combine the yoghurt with the chopped coriander and cayenne, season with salt and freshly ground black pepper, and mix well. Serve the fries with a pot of the yoghurt for dipping, and lime wedges for squeezing over.

VARIATION *Try out flavour combinations by using a Cajun or Jerk seasoning for spiced fries.*

ROASTED BROCCOLI
AND ASPARAGUS
WITH PEANUTS AND SPICY SAUCE

A super-simple dish to serve alongside fried rice or spicy noodles. Use whatever type of broccoli takes your fancy — regular, Tenderstem or even purple sprouting when in season.

SERVES 4

300g trimmed broccoli
250g asparagus, trimmed
1 tbsp sunflower oil
50g peanuts or cashews
  (unsalted)
2 tsp sesame seeds

DRESSING
½ tbsp sunflower oil
1 tsp grated ginger
1 small clove garlic, crushed
2 tbsp soy sauce
1 tbsp chilli sauce
1 tbsp sesame oil

Preheat the oven to 180°C/360°F/gas mark 4.

Arrange the broccoli and asparagus on a baking tray in a single layer, drizzle with 1 tbsp sunflower oil and roast in the oven for 5 minutes. Roughly chop the nuts, tip onto another tray and toast alongside the veg for 2–3 minutes until golden.

Scatter the veg with sesame seeds and roast for another 8–10 minutes until the veg has just started to turn golden and char at the edges.

Meanwhile, prepare the dressing. Spoon the sunflower oil into a small frying pan, add the grated ginger and crushed garlic, and cook over a medium heat for about 30 seconds — just long enough to take the heat out of the garlic but not to brown it. Slide the pan off the heat and add the remaining dressing ingredients.

Pour the dressing over the roasted veggies, scatter with nuts and leave to cool slightly and absorb the flavours before serving.

FENNEL AND SWISS CHARD GRATIN

Taleggio works really well in this dish, but for a vegetarian option, you can try a flavoursome soft-rinded cheese, such as Cornish brie.

SERVES 6 AS A SIDE DISH

500ml double cream
2 cloves garlic, peeled and
   halved
1 bay leaf
2 large or 3 small bulbs
   fennel
10g butter, for greasing
1 bunch Swiss chard
100g taleggio or vegetarian
   soft-rinded cheese, such
   as Cornish brie
2 tbsp breadcrumbs
1 tbsp grated vegetarian
   Italian-style hard cheese
salt and freshly ground
   black pepper

Pour the cream into a small saucepan, add the garlic and bay leaf, and bring to the boil. Remove from the heat and leave to infuse for 30 minutes.

Preheat the oven to 180°C/360°F/gas mark 4.

Trim the fennel and cut into wedges – either 6 or 8 per fennel depending on size. Steam over boiling water for 4–5 minutes or until tender. Use the butter to grease a gratin dish, then remove the fennel from the pan and tip into the buttered dish.

Separate the leaves and stalks from the Swiss chard. Slice the stalks into 3cm pieces, tip into the steamer and cook for 2–3 minutes. Meanwhile slice the leaves and add these to the pan, and cook for a further minute or so until wilted.

Remove from the pan and arrange around the fennel wedges. Season well and strain the infused cream over the veggies. Cut the taleggio into nuggets and tuck amongst the vegetables. Scatter with breadcrumbs and the grated Italian-style hard cheese and bake on the middle shelf of the preheated oven for 30 minutes until golden and bubbling.

KALE PURÉE

This versatile purée has myriad uses. It can be served simply as a side dish, stirred through polenta or mashed potato, or tossed through pasta with a good spoonful of ricotta. It can be made ahead and stored in the fridge or freezer until needed, then warmed and spooned onto toasted bread with a poached egg...

SERVES 2–4

2 cloves garlic, peeled and
    halved
150g whole leaf kale
2–3 tbsp extra-virgin olive
    oil
salt and freshly ground
    black pepper

Fill a large saucepan with salted water, add the garlic cloves and bring to the boil.

Strip the kale from the tough stalks, add to the pan and blanch for 2–3 minutes until tender. Drain though a colander and refresh under running cold water to stop the cooking and to preserve the vibrant green colour of the kale.

Drain the leaves and garlic, squeeze in your hands and pat dry on a clean tea towel to remove as much water as possible.

Tip the kale and garlic into the food processor and blend until nearly smooth, stopping the machine and scraping down the sides of the mixer bowl from time to time. Season the kale purée with salt and freshly ground black pepper.

TIP *Freeze your purée in large-cube silicone ice trays, then pop them out and store in the freezer until needed.*

SMACKED CUCUMBER

VEGAN

This is one of the easiest, quickest and most delicious pickles, and is perfect to serve alongside noodles or fried rice. Look out for chiu chow chilli oil for an authentic Chinese chilli hit — it's available in larger supermarkets or online. Add some chopped salted peanuts and chopped coriander leaves for an extra flavour hit.

SERVES 4–6

1 cucumber
1 tsp salt
1 clove garlic, crushed
1 tsp caster sugar
2 tsp soy sauce
1 tsp rice vinegar
2 tsp chilli oil
1 tsp toasted sesame seeds
(white or a mixture of
black and white seeds)

Place the cucumber on the work surface and smack it 3–4 times evenly down its length with a rolling pin, using enough pressure to just break the skin and loosen the seeds but not to reduce the cucumber to a pulp.

Cut the cucumber into long thin quarters and then across into diagonal slices 2–3cm long. Place the cucumber in a colander, sprinkle with the salt, mix well and leave to drain for 10–15 minutes.

Meanwhile, combine the garlic, sugar, soy, vinegar and chilli oil in a bowl. Shake any excess water from the cucumber and tip into the bowl, mix well to combine with the dressing and leave for a further 5 minutes to absorb the flavours. Transfer to a serving dish, scatter with sesame seeds and serve.

PUTTANESCA CHERRY TOMATOES

These slow-roasted tomatoes are so very versatile. They can be used as a pasta sauce, as a topping for grilled sourdough or spooned on top of soft cheesy polenta.

SERVES 4–6

500g vine cherry tomatoes
3 fat cloves garlic
5 tbsp extra-virgin olive oil
good pinch crushed dried
  chilli flakes
2 large sprigs basil
1–2 tbsp wine vinegar
  (muscatel or sherry
  ideally)
150g mixed pitted olives,
  halved
2 tbsp capers
salt and freshly ground
  black pepper

Preheat the oven to 170°C/350°F/gas mark 4. Line a medium-sized roasting tin or baking tray with baking parchment, making sure that it comes up the sides of the tin.

Place the tomatoes on the tray and tumble the whole, unpeeled garlic cloves around. Drizzle over the olive oil, season with chilli flakes, salt and freshly ground black pepper, and tuck the basil sprigs among the tomatoes. Cook on the middle shelf of the preheated oven for about 20–25 minutes until the tomatoes are tender but not bursting their skins.

Add the remaining ingredients, reduce the oven temperature to 150°C/300°F/gas mark 2 and return to the oven for another 20–30 minutes.

Leave to cool and then serve stirred through pasta, or on top of grilled sourdough or soft polenta.

BLISTERED SUGAR SNAPS
WITH CHILLI AND MINT

SERVES 4

1 red chilli, deseeded and
   finely sliced
2 sprigs mint, shredded
juice of 1 lime
3 tbsp fruity olive oil
250g sugar snap peas
1 fat clove garlic, sliced
salt and freshly ground
   black pepper
sea salt flakes, to serve

Serve these hot and crunchy sugar snap peas as a starter, a side dish or as a sharing plate like tapas — in much the same way as you would padrón peppers.

Combine the sliced chilli, mint, lime juice and 2 tbsp olive oil in a bowl, and season with salt and freshly ground black pepper. Trim the sugar snap peas.

Heat the remaining tablespoon of oil in a large frying pan over a high heat. Add the sliced garlic and cook for 20 seconds to soften. Add the sugar snaps and cook quickly over a high heat, tossing them in the pan, until they blister and lightly char.

Tip onto a serving plate and spoon over the dressing. Season with a pinch of sea salt flakes and serve immediately.

TIP *This simple and quick method of cooking sugar snaps would work just as well with tender broccoli, mangetout or french beans — or indeed a combination of all three.*
Try adding a dash of soy sauce in place of the sea salt flakes, swapping the olive oil for sesame oil and topping with toasted sesame seeds and a scattering of coriander.

POTATO, TOMATO AND ROSEMARY FOCACCIA

This pillowy light bread is topped with cherry tomatoes, garlic, rosemary, salt and a generous glug of fruity olive oil, and it contains a secret ingredient… mashed potato. The starch and natural sugars in the mashed potato and potato cooking water give this bread extra lift and bounce. This bread is perfect for feeding a crowd and serving as part of an Italian feast.

MAKES 1 LARGE LOAF

- 1 large floury potato (such as Maris Piper, about 225–250g), peeled
- 400g strong white bread flour, plus extra for dusting
- 300g '00' flour
- 7g sachet fast-action/easy-bake/easy-blend dried yeast
- ½ tsp fine salt
- 4 tbsp olive oil, plus extra for greasing
- 2–3 tbsp extra-virgin olive oil
- 150g cherry tomatoes, halved
- 2–3 garlic cloves, thinly sliced
- 2 sprigs rosemary, leaves roughly chopped
- 2–3 tsp sea salt flakes
- 30 x 37cm baking tin, with a depth of at least 5cm

Cut the potato into quarters and cook in boiling water until tender all the way through when tested with the point of a knife. Drain, reserving the cooking water, and leave the potato to steam dry for 3–4 minutes. Mash the potato until smooth, and leave to cool. Measure the potato water – you will need 375ml, so add tap water, if needed, to make up the difference.

Tip both types of flour into the bowl of a free-standing mixer fitted with a dough hook, add the yeast and fine salt, and mix with a whisk or spoon to combine. Add the cooled mashed potato and mix again.

Warm the potato water and pour 350ml into the mixing bowl with the olive oil. Mix on medium speed for about 5 minutes until the dough is silky smooth and comes away from the sides of the bowl. It should be a sticky dough, so add a little more water if the mixture seems dry during the initial mixing stage.

Turn the dough onto a floured work surface and use your (wet or floured) hands to shape into a neat ball. Wash and dry the mixing bowl, and brush with a little olive oil. Return the dough to the bowl, rounded side uppermost, cover loosely with a clean tea towel and leave to prove at room temperature for 1 hour.

Brush the baking tin with olive oil. Turn the dough out of the bowl onto a floured work surface and knead briefly to knock out the air bubbles. Scoop the dough into the tin and, using slightly wet or floured hands, press and shape it to fill the tin evenly. Cover with a damp tea towel and set aside to

continues

prove for another 45 minutes to 1 hour, by which time the dough will have risen significantly and be covered in air bubbles.

Preheat the oven to 200°C/400°F/gas mark 6.

Drizzle the top of the bread with the extra-virgin olive oil and, using your fingers, press dimples all over the bread. Scatter the halved cherry tomatoes, sliced garlic and chopped rosemary all over the dough. Sprinkle with sea salt flakes and bake on the middle shelf of the preheated oven for 30 minutes until the bread is well-risen and golden brown.

Leave to cool slightly before cutting into squares or wedges and serving.

TIP *Any leftovers can be sliced, toasted or grilled and topped with chargrilled vegetables, scrambled eggs and wilted greens, or diced and baked into croutons.*

LAZY ROAST POTATOES

Roast potatoes for those that prefer crispy bits and are not too worried about looks. These potatoes should be a bit rough around the edges – the rougher they are the more crispy they'll be. Any leftovers can be stirred into omelettes (see Masala Omelette, page 29) or turned into a potato salad with a light buttermilk dressing, such as the one used for Charred Hispi Cabbage with Buttermilk Dressing, on page 154).

SERVES 4

1kg **Maris Piper potatoes (unpeeled)**
4 tbsp **olive oil**
1 tsp **fennel seeds**
1 tsp **crushed dried chilli flakes**
1 tsp **garlic granules**
sea salt flakes

Preheat the oven to 200°C/400°F/gas mark 6.

Cut the potatoes into quarters and cook in boiling salted water until tender when tested with the point of a small, sharp knife. Drain well through a colander. Shake the colander vigorously to break up and lightly crush the potatoes.

Tip the potatoes into a roasting tin, pour over the olive oil, add the fennel seeds, chilli flakes and garlic granules, and season well with sea salt flakes. Stir well to combine – do not worry about breaking up the potatoes as you stir.

Roast the potatoes on the middle shelf of the preheated oven for about 1 hour, stirring from time to time until the potatoes are really crisp and golden.

CHARRED HISPI CABBAGE
WITH BUTTERMILK DRESSING

This salad is a modern twist on coleslaw — in this instance the cabbage is lightly chargrilled, which brings out its natural sweetness. The dressing is full of flavour, but light and bright — buttermilk is a delicious alternative to mayonnaise. Try adding some shredded Brussels sprouts to the salad when they are in season.

SERVES 4–6

200ml buttermilk
2 tbsp roughly chopped dill
2 tbsp extra-virgin olive oil
1 tbsp tahini
1 clove garlic, crushed
finely grated zest and juice
  of 1 lime
1 hispi cabbage
2 tbsp olive oil
1 mild green chilli,
  deseeded and finely sliced
1 tbsp chopped whole
  almonds
1 tbsp chopped toasted
  pumpkin seeds
1–2 tsp poppy seeds
good pinch sumac
salt and freshly ground
  black pepper

Prepare the dressing before cooking the cabbage to allow time for the flavours to mingle. In a bowl combine the buttermilk, half of the dill, the extra-virgin olive oil, tahini, crushed garlic and a squeeze of lime juice. Season the dressing well with salt and freshly ground black pepper and mix to combine. Cover and chill until ready to serve.

Heat a ridged griddle pan over a medium heat. Remove any tough outer leaves from the cabbage and cut into wedges 4–5cm thick. Brush the cut sides of the cabbage wedges with olive oil and cook on the hot griddle pan for 3–4 minutes on each side until nicely charred and starting to soften. Remove from the pan, arrange on a serving platter and leave to cool slightly.

Spoon the dressing over the cabbage and top with the green chilli, almonds, seeds and reserved dill. Sprinkle with a little sumac and the lime zest and serve.

CONVERSION CHART

WEIGHTS

7.5g	¼oz
15g	½oz
20g	¾oz
30g	1oz
35g	1¼oz
40g	1½oz
50g	1¾oz
55g	2oz
60g	2¼oz
70g	2½oz
80g	2¾oz
85g	3oz
90g	3¼oz
100g	3½oz
115g	4oz
125g	4½oz
140g	5oz
150g	5½oz
170g	6oz
185g	6½oz
200g	7oz
225g	8oz
250g	9oz
285g	10oz
300g	10½oz
310g	11oz
340g	12oz
370g	13oz
400g	14oz
425g	15oz
450g	1lb
500g	1lb 2oz
565g	1¼ lb
680g	1½ lb
700g	1lb 9oz
750g	1lb 10oz
800g	1¾ lb
900g	2lb
1kg	2lb 3oz
1.1kg	2lb 7oz
1.4kg	3lb
1.5kg	3½lb
1.8kg	4lb
2kg	4½lb
2.3kg	5lb
2.7kg	6lb
3.1kg	7lb
3.6kg	8lb
4.5kg	10lb

VOLUME

5ml	1 teaspoon	
10ml	1 dessertspoon	
15ml	1 tablespoon	
30ml	1fl oz	
40ml	1½fl oz	
55ml	2fl oz	
70ml	2½fl oz	
85ml	3fl oz	
100ml	3½ fl oz	
120ml	4fl oz	
130ml	4½fl oz	
150ml	5fl oz	
170ml	6fl oz	
185ml	6½fl oz	
200ml	7fl oz	
225ml	8fl oz	
250ml	9fl oz	
270ml	9½fl oz	
285ml	10fl oz	½ pint
300ml	10½fl oz	
345ml	12fl oz	
400ml	14fl oz	
425ml	15fl oz	¾ pint
450ml	16fl oz	
465ml	16½fl oz	
500ml	18fl oz	
565ml	20fl oz	1 pint
700ml	25fl oz	1¼ pints
750ml	26fl oz	
850ml	30fl oz	1½ pints
1 litre	35fl oz	1¾ pints
1.2 litres	42fl oz	2 pints
1.5 litres	53fl oz	2½ pints
2 litres	70fl oz	3½ pints

All eggs are medium unless stated otherwise. Use either metric or imperial measures, not a mixture of the two.

LENGTH

5mm	¼in
1cm	½in
2cm	¾in
2.5cm	1in
6cm	2½in
7cm	2¾in
7.5cm	3in
9cm	3½in
10cm	4in
18cm	7in
20cm	8in
22cm	8½in
23cm	9in
25cm	10in
28cm	11in
30cm	12in
35cm	14in
38cm	15in

OVEN TEMPERATURES

DESCRIPTION	FAN	CONVENTIONAL	GAS
Very cool	100°C	110°C/225°F	Gas ¼
Very cool	120°C	120°C/250°F	Gas ½
Cool	130°C	140°C/275°F	Gas 1
Slow	140°C	150°C/300°F	Gas 2
Moderately slow	150°C	160°C/320°F	Gas 3
Moderately slow	160°C	170°C/325°F	Gas 3
Moderate	170°C	180°C/360°F	Gas 4
Moderately hot	180°C	190°C/375°F	Gas 5
Hot	190°C	200°C/400°F	Gas 6
Very hot	200°C	220°C/425°F	Gas 7
Very hot	220°C	230°C/450°F	Gas 8
Hottest	230°C	240°C/475°F	Gas 9

INDEX